RADIE BRITAIN

Radie Britain, circa 1950. Photo by Seawell, courtesy Radie Britain.

RADIE BRITAIN

A Bio-Bibliography

Walter B. Bailey
and
Nancy Gisbrecht Bailey

Bio-Bibliographies in Music, Number 25
Donald L. Hixon, Series Adviser

GREENWOOD PRESS
New York • Westport, Connecticut • London

Library of Congress Cataloging-in-Publication Data

Bailey, Walter B. (Walter Boyce)
  Radie Britain : a bio-bibliography / Walter B. Bailey and Nancy
Gisbrecht Bailey.
    p. cm.—(Bio-bibliographies in music, ISSN 0742-6968 ; no.
25)
  Includes bibliographical references.
  ISBN 0-313-26277-2 (alk. paper)
  1. Britain, Radie, 1903-   —Bibliography. I. Bailey, Nancy
Gisbrecht. II. Title. III. Series.
ML134.B845B3   1990
780'.92—dc20
  [B]   89-78117

British Library Cataloguing in Publication Data is available.

Library of Congress Catalog Card Number: 89-78117
ISBN: 0-313-26277-2
ISSN: 0742-6968

First published in 1990

Greenwood Press, 88 Post Road West, Westport, CT 06881
An imprint of Greenwood Publishing Group, Inc.

Printed in the United States of America

The paper used in this book complies with the
Permanent Paper Standard issued by the National
Information Standards Organization (Z39.48-1984).

10 9 8 7 6 5 4 3 2 1

To Radie Britain

Contents

Preface

The purpose of this volume is to provide access to materials of interest for performers and scholars concerning the prolific American composer Radie Britain. To that end it is divided into several parts. First, a short biography summarizes the major events of Miss Britain's life and the conditions under which she evolved as a musician. Second, an interview allows Miss Britain to comment on the distinctive qualities of her life, music, and creative philosophy. An exhaustive list of works and performances follows, including significant information about each work, documented performances, and the source from which musicians may obtain scores (addresses and lending information are included in the list of libraries, archives, and publishers following this Preface). Concluding the body of the text is a chronological bibliography of Miss Britain's writings, with pertinent quotations from each, and a similarly-enriched bibliography of reviews of performances of Miss Britain's works and other press materials concerning her career. It is hoped that the chronological arrangement of the bibliography will cause it to read like a second biography. Appendices include chronological and alphabetical lists of her works. An index to the entire volume is also included. Since only one of Miss Britain's works has been recorded professionally (the *Prelude to a Drama* recorded by the United States Air Force Symphony Orchestra and distributed at military PX's throughout the world) and since that recording was not made available to the general public, the "Discography" typically included in the books of this series has been omitted.

The various sections of the book are related to one another by means of two numbering systems. Each work in the "Works and Performances" section, for example, is assigned an identifying number prefaced by the letter "W" (for "Work"). Each performance of a given work is then assigned an alphabet letter, so that, by way of demonstration, the first performance of the first work in the list is labeled "W1a" and the third performance of the second work in the list is labeled "W2c." Works and specific performances of works are referred to in this manner throughout the text.

Similarly, each entry in the Bibliography is assigned a number prefaced by the letter "B," for Bibliography. Cross references link specific pieces with reviews of those pieces, and vice versa.

This volume could not have been completed without Radie Britain's assistance. Miss Britain provided the authors with a list of her works, the instrumentation of orchestral works (presented here in the usual format with numbers indicating the required wind and brass instruments), dates of performances of which she was aware, lists of prizes awarded to her, copies of her writings, and lists of her musical affiliations. She also generously provided access to her several scrapbooks, large volumes filled with newspaper and periodical clippings, often attached without indication of city, newspaper, date or author. Of invaluable assistance was the loan of her unpublished autobiography, an artistically conceived memoire intentionally vague regarding dates but rich with insight into a wonderfully creative life. Miss Britain herself is an ebullient inspiration to life and music, and we are grateful for the opportunity of meeting her and working with her music.

It was the authors' task to track down information missing or unverified in Miss Britain's records and to supplement it with material from other sources. Regarding the list of works, we discovered references to a number of pieces attributed to Miss Britain which were not a part of her records. In some cases Miss Britain was happy to acknowledge these lost compositions; in others she declined to include them in her catalog. Following her lead, we have omitted works mentioned in reviews but not acknowledged by the composer. In the Bibliography, the degree of our success in locating and verifying material is indicated by the relative completeness or incompleteness of specific bibliographical entries. Unfortunately, many of the items in Miss Britain's scrapbooks could not be dated exactly or attributed to a specific source: these items were omitted unless they were especially pertinent. Incomplete citations for these entries include material in brackets ("[ ]") conjectured by the authors on the basis of available information. A review of a performance in Chicago probably (but not always) appeared in a Chicago newspaper; reviews usually (but not always) appeared soon after the performance; items penned by a specific author usually (but not always) appeared in the newspaper which employed the author at the time. To compensate for the occasional lack of a complete citation, it has been our practice to include substantial quotations from the printed reviews.

By employing Miss Britain's record of performances we were able to discover a number of reviews unknown to her, but we also found that a significant number of her works had not been reviewed. Often, in large cities with multiple concerts and limited newspaper space, the performances of new works have been bypassed for reviews of traditional concerts that attract a larger audience. In the smaller cities, it seems that, traditionally, musical performances are not reviewed. Miss Britain's more recent works have suffered from these situations and other special circumstances. For example, her description of the point at which she felt she reached the pinnacle of her career, a performance held in Detroit in 1961, occurred simultaneously with a newspaper strike that precluded a review of this significant event.

In creating this volume we have been assisted by several helpful individuals. In addition to the staff of Rice University's Interlibrary Loan department, Linda Chelf of Amarillo, Timothy Verner of Chicago, and Susan Moore of New York have helped to locate materials and information central to the accuracy and completeness of the work. Tom Littman of the Shepherd School of Music was especially generous with printing assistance. We thank them and the staffs of the libraries, archives, and publishers included in the list following this Preface for their help.

Houston, Texas
August 1989

Directory of Libraries, Archives, and Publishers

Amarillo Public Library
P.O. Box 2171
Amarillo, Texas 79189-2171

American Heritage Center
Twentieth-Century Music Collection
University of Wyoming
Laramie, Wyoming 82071

American Music Center
2109 Broadway, Suite 1579
New York, New York 10023

American Music Edition
c/o Theodore Presser Company
Presser Place
Bryn Mawr, Pennsylvania 19010

Harold Branch Publishing, Inc.
87 Eads Street
West Babylon, New York 11704

California State University Dominguez Hills
Music Library
1000 E. Victoria
Carson, California 90747

Carson County Square House Museum
P.O. Box 276
Panhandle, Texas 79068

Carl Fischer, Inc.
62 Cooper Square
New York, New York 10003

The Edwin A. Fleisher Collection of Orchestral Music
The Free Library of Philadelphia
Logan Square
Philadelphia, Pennsylvania 19103

Heroico Music Publications
1945 North Curson Avenue
Hollywood, California 90046

Neil A. Kjos Music Co.
4382 Jutland Drive
San Diego, California 92117

The Moldenhauer Collection at Harvard University
The Houghton Library
Harvard University
Cambridge, Massachusetts 02138

Opus Music Publishers, Inc.
1880 Holste Road
Northbrook, Illinois 60062

Ossian Music Publisher
c/o Music Sales Corporation
24 E. 22nd Street
New York, New York 10010

Ricordi and Sons/Ricordi and Sons, Brazil
c/o Hal Leonard Publishing Corporation
7777 West Bluemound Road
Box 18319
Milwaukee, Wisconsin 53213

San Francisco Conservatory
1201 Ortega Street
San Francisco, California 94122

Seesaw Music Corporation
2067 Broadway
New York, New York 10023

Clayton F. Summy/Summy-Birchard
c/o Birch Tree Group, Ltd.
180 Alexander Street
Princeton, New Jersey 08540

Texas Composers Collection
Eugene C. Barker Texas History Center
SRH 2.109
The University of Texas at Austin
Austin, Texas 78713-7330

Texas Federation of Music Clubs Music Manuscript Archives
Fine Arts Division, Dallas Public Library
1515 Young Street
Dallas, Texas 75201

Trombone Association Publications
662 Riverdale Street
West Springfield, Massachussets 01089

UCLA Music Library Archival Collection
(The Radie Britain Collection)
Music Library
University of California, Los Angeles
Los Angeles, California 90024

Willis Music Company
7380 Industrial Road
Florence, Kentucky 41042

Witmark and Sons
c/o Warner Bros. Publications
265 Secaucus Road
Secaucus, New Jersey 07094

RADIE BRITAIN

Biography

Radie Britain, a native of West Texas, studied piano and composition in Chicago and Munich before her debut as a composer in 1926. As a woman in a male-dominated field, she faced considerable obstacles in the pursuit and practice of her calling, and she surmounted them with the optimism characteristic of her approach to life. The highest concentration of performances of her works occurred in Chicago in the 1930s and 1940s, and she has continued to the present day to enjoy many performances in Los Angeles and other cities around the world. Her music is inspired, well-crafted, and conservative (by twentieth-century avant-garde standards). It has been and continues to be warmly received by critics and audiences alike.

Radie Britain was born on a ranch near Silverton, in the Panhandle region of Texas, on March 17, 1899. Her parents, Katie Ford Britain (1873-1957) and Edgar Charles Britain (1869-1962), both natives of Dallas, were pioneer settlers of West Texas. Edgar had come to the recently-tamed region around 1884 as a horse wrangler. He remained there as a cow hand at the JA Ranch, which had been founded in 1877 by Charles Goodnight and John George Adair, the first permanent white settlers of the area. He returned to Dallas to marry Katie Ford in 1891, and the couple home-steaded a section of land in Swisher County about forty-five miles from Amarillo.[1]

By the time of Radie's birth, the Britain family had traded their home-stead for a ranch in Briscoe County, and Radie grew up taking the realities of frontier ranch-life for granted. Every so often, for example, the family travelled by horse-drawn wagon to Amarillo or Clarendon, a small town on the line of the Fort Worth and Denver railroad, to purchase supplies which they could not produce on their own.

As the third of five children, Radie held a very special position in her family. Since the Britain's first child, a girl named Zadie, had died of dipth-eria in infancy, and since their second child, Roy, was several years Radie's senior, Radie's birth was met with great attention. Her father found her especially appealing and doted on her for the rest of his life. Her mother, always seeking for her children the advantages which she had been denied, demanded the best from Radie, and encouraged her to expand her boundaries. The Britains had great aspirations for all of their children, Roy, Radie, their younger brother, Edgar, and their younger sister, Bonnie Marie. Bonnie Marie died in her teens, but the other children excelled in their chosen fields.

In 1905, to foster the education of their children, the Britains traded their ranch near Silverton for one located in Clarendon where they would be close to Clarendon College, a Methodist junior college founded in 1898.[2] In town, Radie took piano lessons with Miss Wedgewood, a graduate of the Dresden Conservatory. Her mother, especially, took Radie's lessons very seriously, and Radie was required to practice for several hours a day before being allowed any social privileges. Her playing was praised, and she was held up as a model musician in the community.

Radie's parents had differing musical backgounds. Her father knew many "cowboy" songs and could play square dance tunes on the fiddle, a talent apparently developed before his conversion to strict Methodism. Her mother had taken a limited number of music lessons in her youth and played religious songs on a pump organ in the Britain home. Both of her parents were enthusiastic about Radie's musical progress. Eventually, when threatened with the prospect of no lessons for the summer, Radie took on the task of regulating her own practice time and never had to be forced or even reminded to practice again.

Radie's playing progressed rapidly, and, by about 1911, she had begun piano lessons at Clarendon College with R. Deane Shure, a graduate of the Leipzig Conservatory. Dr. Shure had great hopes for Radie and he advised her that she could have a fine musical career if she did not marry too early, advice that guided her for many years. Her lessons were held at 7:30 in the morning to accommodate her high school studies, which were further enriched by Radie's participation in high school dramatic presentations. By the time that she was fifteen, Radie had joined her teacher's advanced students in a harmony class at the college.

Just prior to the beginning of her senior year (1917), Radie's parents traded their ranch near Clarendon for one in the Palo Duro Canyon, twenty miles from Amarillo. They also purchased a lot in Amarillo, where they built an opulent, two-story brick home. To complete her musical studies at the college and her senior year of high school, Radie stayed on in Clarendon, where she resided in the college dormitory and was supervised by the college staff.

For her senior recital, Radie performed a Bach Prelude and Fugue, Liszt's Hungarian Rhapsody Number 12, and Chopin's Military Polonaise. She found new freedom in life away from home, despite the strict regulations of the college. Male and female students were not allowed to socialize or even talk together at Clarendon College and dancing was strictly forbidden. Before leaving the college, Radie had been punished for breaking both of these rules.

Her rebellion against the rules of the college was an expression of her lack of sympathy for the ultra-conservative qualities of Methodism. The long hours that she spent in church and the revival meetings which she was forced to attend seemed unnatural to her, as did the general prohibition of dancing. But the consistent religious tone of her upbringing created a strong faith which transcended strict Methodism and remains the foundation of her religious life.

Miss Radie Britain spent the summer following her graduation (1918) trying to convince her parents that she should pursue further musical study at a conservatory in one of the larger Eastern cities. To fuel her argument she ordered catalogs from conservatories in Chicago, Boston, and Cincinnati. It was her greatest wish to hear live performances of large-scale musical events and to associate with major musical figures. Although her mother was supportive, her father believed that her academic career had ended with her first diploma. He enjoyed having her at home with him and did not want her to leave Texas, stating that a good education could be had in her home state.

In the course of the summer she was approached by the staff of Crescent College in Arkansas, a finishing school attended by about one hundred young women from the southern states. Although, initially, she did not want to settle for anything less than a major conservatory in a large, culturally mature city, Miss Britain began to see that if she gained permission to travel the short distance outside of Texas to Arkansas for a year, it would make it easier for her father to accept her eventual wish to study further away from home. Miss Britain enrolled in the college in the fall of 1918.

At Crescent College, located near Eureka Springs, Miss Britain studied piano and organ with Dr. Arthur Sherubel, who immediately recognized her talent. Like her earlier teacher, Professor Sherubel advised her that she could have a fine career if she did not marry too young. Her studies progressed rapidly and at the end of the school year she received her diploma. Her senior recital included works of Bach, Mendelssohn, Beethoven, and Chopin.

Upon returning to her parents' home in Amarillo at the conclusion of the school year, Miss Britain found that her mother had convinced her father of the need for further study at a conservatory. Although she would have preferred to go to the Boston Conservatory, since she knew a young woman who attended Wellesley College, her father had selected the American Conservatory of Chicago, believing that she would have fewer distractions from her studies in a city where she was a stranger. Miss Britain acquiesced to her father's wishes. She had always had an active social life and knew that she could win friends wherever she traveled. She also knew that her father's concern about distractions from her studies were unfounded. Many of her friends in Amarillo were marrying, but she had decided that her career was her first priority.

That fall, Professor Sherubel met her at the conservatory in Chicago to help her determine her teachers and schedule. Following his advice, she selected Heniot Levy for piano, Frank Van Dusen for organ, Arthur Olaf Andersen for counterpoint, Louise Robyn for pedagogy, and Stella Roberts for ensemble. Miss Britain was impressed with the size and scope of Chicago, as well as its musical life. Her first orchestral concert, with Frederick Stock leading the Chicago Symphony Orchestra in Beethoven's Fifth Symphony, left a lasting impression. Finally, she was realizing the goals that she had set for herself.

Miss Britain concentrated on her piano studies, but her undemonstrative piano teacher made it difficult for her to measure her progress. Only in December did he inform her that she was one of his best pupils, and that she would be eligible for a teacher's certificate at the end of the school year. In addition to addressing her piano studies, Miss Britain attended many concerts, and she began to be interested in composition. She felt unsure of her own creations, however, and did not show them to her teachers. She engaged in an active social life and was pursued by a young doctor who was interested in marriage, but she was relieved when the relationship did not develop.

For her final examination Miss Britain played a group of pieces including a Bach Prelude and Fugue and an Intermezzo by Saint-Saëns. The climate of the exams was grueling, much more so than in any of her previous experiences. But Miss Britain's dedication was rewarded: she won "Special Honorable Mention" in piano, a "Gold Medal" in organ, and "Honorable Mention" in pedagogy.

Upon returning to Amarillo, Miss Britain found that, once again, her father assumed that her academic career was over, since she had received another diploma (a teacher's certificate). On the contrary, Miss Britain had determined that she would return to Chicago for a second year, to complete her Bachelor of Music degree, and then go on to study in Europe. Eventually she obtained her father's consent, and she returned to Chicago in the fall of 1920 for her second year at the conservatory.

Miss Britain's second year of studies progressed well, and to her performing responsibilities she added teacher's training, which she applied at Jane Addams' Hull House in an underprivileged area of Chicago. Although shocked by the degree of poverty which she observed there, Miss Britain hoped that her musical instruction might inspire a small degree of hope in her young students.

Miss Britain's primary energies were directed toward her piano studies, but she was becoming dissatisfied with the performer's lot. In a competition to select a soloist to perform with the Chicago Symphony Orchestra at the conservatory's commencement exercises, Miss Britain played the first movement of the Grieg Piano Concerto. Due to a technical error in her performance, she did not win the competition. More and more, her thoughts turned toward the creative processes of composition, as opposed to the re-creative process of the performer.

Miss Britain was awarded her Bachelor of Music degree in the spring of 1921, but stayed on in Chicago for the summer to audit the master classes of Leopold Godowsky and visit the master classes of Josef Lhevinne. She would have liked to have played for these teachers, but, perhaps as the result of exercises given to her by her teacher at the conservatory, she was experiencing neuritis in her forearms.

Despite her strict Methodist upbringing, Miss Britain followed a friend's advice in seeking aid from a Christian Science practitioner to ease the pain of her neuritis. The treatment did not cure her completely, but it supported many of the metaphysical, optimistic traits that she had been developing in her personal philosophy for some time. The Christian Science idea of using positive imagery to achieve physical results went along with

Miss Britain's optimistic outlook on life, and the idea of becoming one with the power of God was already familiar to her through performing and listening to music. Although the neuritis was painful, it had the positive influence of focussing her attentions on the development of her personal philosophy and on aspects of music other than performance, especially composition.

Upon graduating, Miss Britain sought a teaching position so that she could earn and save enough money for a trip to Europe and additional musical study. Although she had no intention of returning immediately to Texas, a job opening at Clarendon College, and her father's fervent wish that she seek employment in her home state, lured her back to her alma mater. For the fee of one hundred dollars a month, plus room and board, she accepted the position of teacher of piano and music history, organist of the Methodist church, and sports director of the girls' basketball and tennis teams. Although she had hoped that it would be otherwise, she found that the strict rules applied to her as a student were still in place at the college, and that they were applied with equal vigor to the faculty. Even before taking up her post in the fall, reports of her social dancing in Amarillo jeopardized her position. At the end of the year she was happy to decline an offer to continue teaching there for a second year.

During the summer of 1922, Miss Britain studied in Dallas with the Italian organist Pietro Yon at the then exorbitant fee of fifty dollars an hour. She justified the expense with the knowledge that her insight and technique were improving beyond her expectations. In the fall she set up a private studio in Amarillo, teaching piano to many children and saving the proceeds for her proposed study in Europe.

At this point in time, the prospect of a career in music was so attractive that she consciously avoided romantic commitment, despite the availability of prospective suitors. With her parents' understanding she made the "sacrifices" that she believed were typically required of artists early on in their careers. In her own assessment of her situation, she made a conscious choice between marriage and a career.

In the summer of 1923, Miss Britain made her first trip to Europe. With her mother's support and her father's reluctant consent, she sailed from New York to Bordeaux and then travelled on to Paris. To aid in her cultural immersion, she lived in a pension where only French was spoken. It was her intention to study there for two months, but she had not worked out the details of her instruction before leaving the United States. From Isidore Phillip's secretary she learned that she would have to master Phillip's technical system before having lessons with him, so she began her studies with Mademoiselle Du Barry, one of his associates. In her attempts to obtain lessons with Marcel Dupré she was more fortunate, but she could not have as many lessons with him as she wished because of his vacation trips away from Paris. Her lessons with Dupré were very successful, however, and she was also able to observe his playing at the Cathedral of Notre Dame.

Miss Britain actively absorbed French culture, visiting famous locales such as Versailles, the Louvre, and Rodin's studio, which was especially appealing to her. But in a general artistic sense and especially from a musical standpoint, she began to feel that her tastes ran more toward a German sensibility. French music seemed shallow to her in comparison with German music, and she became aware of her special responsiveness to the music of composers such as Mozart, Beethoven, Brahms, and Wagner. To end her stay in Europe, she embarked on a three-week tour of Italy, observing the great art works of Milan, Florence, Venice, Rome, and Naples.

By the time of her return to Amarillo, Miss Britain had refined her plans for the immediate future: she would teach privately for a year, save her money, and go to Germany to study composition. Her year at home, which went much as she had planned, was marked with many musical events sponsored by the city's various musical clubs. Miss Britain also had the opportunity of meeting a number of visiting artists who concertized in Amarillo, including Metropolitan Opera star May Peterson, who later settled in Amarillo.

Prior to her departure, in the fall of 1924, Miss Britain had several contacts in Germany. In Berlin, her first destination, two of her fellow pianists from the American Conservatory were studying piano with Adele aus der Ohre, with whom Miss Britain began lessons. Miss Britain's piano studies proceeded nicely, but, because of her inability to speak German, she found theoretical instruction more difficult. The concert life of the city, however, was easily within her grasp, and she enjoyed performances by soloists, the opera, and the symphony.

Another friend from the American Conservatory, soprano Leone Krause, was under contract with the Munich opera. When Miss Britain went to hear her premiere in *Tosca,* she was introduced to Dr. Albert Noelte (1885-1946), a composer and the music critic of the Munich and Augsburg *Abendzeitung,* who invited her to play her compositions for him. Miss Britain had written only a handful of piano pieces, all of them of fairly recent vintage, and she had never shown them to anyone. But Dr. Noelte, a former student of the Boston Conservatory who spoke English very well, was so impressed with Miss Britain and her compositions that he offered to make her his protégé. Given Noelte's stature in Munich, his musical background, and his ability to speak English, Miss Britain could not refuse such an opportunity, despite her concern that it might be her physical attributes more than her compositions that attracted him.

Once in Munich she proved herself a promising compositional talent and stood fast in her professional relationship with Dr. Noelte. Through Noelte she began to appreciate a metaphysical method of composition, which involved "uncovering" melodies through an unconscious process, and then using all aspects of her compositional technique to create a proper setting for the melody. At Noelte's insistence, she spent days alone in the forest absorbing the "vibrations of nature," something she had never done before. This, in turn, fostered a sense of divine inspiration which she has nurtured and relied on ever since in her creative process.

Through Noelte's influence Miss Britain became familiar with the operas of Wagner and the writings of Schopenhauer, which she welcomed as additions to her metaphysical philosophies. Noelte also introduced her to musicians such as Richard Strauss, whom Miss Britain admired for his powers of orchestration, and the pianist Joseph Pembauer, with whom Miss Britain began to study pieces such as Schubert's *Wanderer* Fantasy. Miss Britain felt as if she had finally found her true calling, and Dr. Noelte assured her that she had the talent to succeed, if she could provide the stamina, which, because she was a woman, would have to be exceptional.

In the spring of 1925 Miss Britain took a break from her studies in Munich to vacation in England and visit a Contemporary Composers' Symposium in London. In general, she was not impressed with the avant-garde music presented there, which she found to be uninspired and largely incomprehensible. Back in Munich, Dr. Noelte predicted that she would be mature enough as a composer for a public performance of her works the following fall.

Miss Britain returned to Amarillo that summer and was widely acclaimed by the local music clubs. After renewing ties with her family and friends, she resumed her studies in Munich in the fall. She sailed to Germany via Norway, where, while visiting Grieg's home, she made a reverent pledge to herself to become one of the world's greatest woman composers.

In Munich she composed the *Western* Suite for piano [W83], which Dr. Noelte convinced the music publisher Otto Halbreiter to publish along with the Prelude for piano [W82]. Knowing that she enjoyed Hungarian gypsy music, which she had heard performed in open air restaurants, Noelte had suggested that she use the cowboy songs and Indian rhythms of America to flavor her compositions. In Noelte's view, the native music of one's homeland was an intrinsic part of a composer's heritage and, thus, should be valued and used. Her relationship with Noelte was strained when she engaged in an active social life that did not include him, but he continued to guide her musically.

In May of 1926, Miss Britain enjoyed her debut as a composer when Erik Wildhagen, a baritone with the Munich Opera and friend of Dr. Noelte, performed four of her songs in recital, accompanied by Miss Britain. The reception of the works was enthusiastic; one song even had to be repeated. The press reviews were lavish, praising the quality of the songs and the promise of the composer. (See: W210, W212, W213, and W215 and B12-B17 and B24-25.) Halbreiter also agreed to publish the songs. Riding the crest of her achievement, Miss Britain immersed herself in her work, but a mere two weeks after her success she received word from Amarillo that her younger sister had died unexpectedly at age thirteen.

Torn with grief and believing that it was her duty to ease her parents' sorrow, she returned to Amarillo. Dr. Noelte, sensitive to her current state of mind and to her potential as a composer, promised that he would continue her instruction in the United States if Miss Britain were unable to return to Munich. During the summer Miss Britain came to realize that it was her duty, as a creative artist, to write music. She vowed that her compositions would be a monument to her own life so that, after her death, her ideas of beauty and art could still be communicated to the world.

In the late summer Miss Britain returned to Chicago, where she had agreed to meet Dr. Noelte. For the next year she remained in Chicago, studying with Noelte, composing, teaching, and performing her own works. After teaching privately in Amarillo during June and July of the next summer (1927), she once again returned to Chicago to meet Noelte. Having fulfilled his commitments in Germany, he became a permanent resident of Chicago, where he and Miss Britain were employed at the Girvin Institute of Music and Allied Arts, headed by Ramon Girvin, who had taught violin at the American Conservatory during Miss Britain's studies there. Dr. Noelte was the head of the composition department, and Miss Britain assisted him as well as teaching piano. Noelte was eventually engaged as the head of the composition department at Northwestern University.

Miss Britain began work on her first orchestral score, *Symphonic Intermezzo* [W2], in 1927. Aided by her knowledge of the organ, she excelled at her work, and soon began a second orchestral composition, an Overture to *Pygmalion* [W1]. *Symphonic Intermezzo*, performed by Ethel Leginska and the Chicago Woman's Orchestra in January 1928, met with wide approval.

Other orchestral works and performances soon followed. The *Heroic Poem* [W3] (1929) won the Juilliard National Publication Prize in 1930 and was performed by Howard Hanson and the Rochester Philharmonic Orchestra in 1932. In 1933 it was played by the Chicago Philharmonic. Miss Britain, inspired by the heroic scope of Charles Lindbergh's recent trans-Atlantic flight to Paris, composed it along the lines of Strauss's tone poems, which she admired greatly.

Miss Britain was one of many composers to benefit from the aggressive programming of new works dictated by the Federal Music Project of the Works Project Administration. The Illinois Symphony Orchestra, for example, an ensemble that played several of her works in the 1930s, was sponsored by the WPA. The *Rhapsodic Phantasie* for piano and orchestra [W4] (1933) was performed by the Illinois Symphony Orchestra in 1938, and in 1940 the same group programmed the *Southern Symphony* [W9] (1935), a four-movement work which includes several traditional Southern melodies. The second movement (Adagio), dedicated by Miss Britain to her father, is based on a cowboy song.

In a performance by Albert Goldberg and the Illinois Symphony Orchestra in January 1937, her second orchestral work, the Overture to *Pygmalion*, was premiered ten years after its inception. In 1938 it was performed by Frederick Stock and the Chicago Symphony Orchestra under its final title, *Prelude to a Drama*. When approached by Dr. Noelte, Stock had agreed to program Miss Britain's work, but he felt that a sensuous subject like *Pygmalion* was inappropriate for the only available opening on the Symphony's calendar, Good Friday. On that particular program its companions would be two organ works of J.S. Bach, transcribed for orchestra, excerpts from Wagner's *Parsifal*, Debussy's *Le martyre de Saint Sebastien*, and excerpts from Vincent d'Indy's *La légende de Saint Christophe*. With Miss Britain's reluctant approval, the work was retitled and program notes were created indicating that the work was modeled on Schiller's *Resurrection*. In the ensuing years, the *Prelude to a Drama* has become Miss Britain's most frequently performed work. It represents the essence of her early musical style, with its Germanic insistence on motivic unity, its Straussian melodic *Schwung*, and its lush Romantic harmonic language.

Other orchestral works by Miss Britain performed at this time include *Light* [W7] (1935), dedicated to Thomas Edison and premiered by the Chicago Woman's Symphony in 1938, *Nocturn* for chamber orchestra [W5] (1934), performed by the Chicago Woman's Concert Ensemble in 1940, and the *Infant Suite* [W6] (1935), which accumulated several performances (including radio broadcasts) in Los Angeles, New York, Chicago, and Amarillo between 1936 and 1941. In 1935 and 1936 Miss Britain resided at the prestigious MacDowell Colony at the recommendation of Amy (Mrs. H. H. A.) Beach.

In securing performances from male conductors who otherwise might not have taken a woman composer seriously, Dr. Noelte acted as Miss Britain's advocate. In other cases, Miss Britain took advantage of her powerful but ambiguous first name. For example, Howard Hanson, never having met Miss Britain, addressed his correspondence concerning the *Heroic Poem* and the Juilliard Publication Prize to Mr. Radie Britain. Dr. Hanson's assumptions regarding Miss Britain's gender may have increased her chances of winning the Juilliard Publication Prize, since she was the first woman to win that award.

In addition to her orchestral works, Miss Britain enjoyed the public reception of a number of other compositions, including the *Epic Poem* for string quartet [W43] (1927), later retitled *Portrait of Thomas Jefferson*, the piano and violin duo *Prison (Lament)* [W47] (1935), and assorted vocal and choral works. *Epic Poem* was performed at the White House in 1936 after it won an award from the National League of American Pen Women.

When it became clear that her career was underway, Miss Britain ignored the one consistent piece of advice that she had received from the beginning of her musical studies: in June of 1930 she married Leslie Edward Moeller, a very successful paper salesman ten years her senior. Moeller was completely wrapped up in his business and had no interest in music, so Miss Britain was left largely on her own and continued to focus on her compositional career. In this she had ample stimulation from outside her marriage, as she continued to consult with Dr. Noelte and a large circle of musicians in Chicago. At first she was satisfied with this arrangement, but she gradually became unhappy with the lack of understanding and artistic support shown by her husband.

When, in the spring of 1931, Miss Britain found herself pregnant, she was forced to focus on the unfavorable qualities of her marriage. When her daughter, Lerae, was born on 15 February 1932, Miss Britain threw herself into imbuing the child with culture, while maintaining her active level in Chicago's musical community.

Amid the professional successes of the 1930s came an event that would rock Miss Britain's personal life: her meeting with Edgardo Simone (1889-1949), the outspoken and irreverent Italian sculptor whom Miss Britain likened to Rodin. Their meeting and eventual courtship, which was worthy of Hollywood cinematic treatment, began when Simone addressed a performance of one of Miss Britain's works with a loud "bravo," the first such acclamation that Miss Britain had received. When they later met, there was an immediate artistic sympathy between them, nurtured through their mutual admiration for one another's works.

In a number of meetings, including social visits with her husband to Simone's studio, sittings for her daughter Lerae's medallion portrait, and sittings for her own portrait bust, Miss Britain was able to exchange ideas with Simone about the artist's creative process. On one occasion she took down a melody whistled by Simone, which he had remembered from a shepherd's pipe song heard on a fishing trip to Wisconsin. At his suggestion, she created an orchestral work from it, the *Pastorale* [W13], which marked the beginnings of a strong bond between them. Simone then created a sculpture inspired by Miss Britain's music.

In Simone's company, Miss Britain and Lerae attended an exhibition of Italian Master paintings at the Chicago Art Institute, further extending their mutual admiration for the arts. He conceived an idea for a piece based on the orgiastic rituals of Bacchus, which he termed *Saturnale* [W14], and Miss Britain set about giving it musical life. Dr. Noelte had obtained a rehearsal with the Chicago Symphony for the work without having seen the score, and was gravely shocked at the change in Miss Britain's style. The "Latin" origins of the work were especially apparent in its rhythmic vitality and Italianate melodies.

In the course of their developing relationship, Miss Britain compared Simone to her husband, to her husband's detriment. In the spring of 1939 she rented a cabin near Ontonagon in upper Michigan and retired there with Lerae to reflect and compose. Inspired by her surroundings, she created the *Ontonagon Sketches* [W12]. When she was visited by her husband and Simone simultaneously, a potentially serious confrontation developed between the two men, and both left. In a letter sent from California, Simone stated that he could no longer live near Miss Britain as long as she was married to her husband, and he invited Miss Britain to join him in California as his wife. After careful consideration, she made the momentous decision to divorce her husband.

Miss Britain preferred to use the charge of desertion for her divorce, which entailed a wait of nine months. She maintained a constant correspondence with Simone, but planned to wait some time before marrying him so that the cause of her separation from her husband would not be so obvious, especially to her parents. Her departure from Chicago for Amarillo when the divorce was finalized late in 1939 was quiet, and few of her circle there were given any explanation for it. Her long-time mentor, Dr. Noelte, had recently married a singer whom he had been coaching. He died in 1946 at age 61.

After visiting Amarillo Miss Britain and Lerae travelled to Coronado, California, where Simone had rented a house in preparation for their arrival. Despite her intentions not to marry right away, a housing shortage in the San Diego area made marriage expedient. In order to save them any embarrassment, she did not tell her parents of her marriage, but, when they eventually learned of it, they were supportive. Miss Britain's musical inspiration was unleashed by her new marriage, resulting in works such as the *Serenada del Coronado* [W91] (1940), *Saint Francis of Assisi* [W17] (1941), and *San Luis Rey* [W18] (1941). At times the marriage was personally explosive, but it was always ripe with artistic inspiration.

Miss Britain and Simone gathered students and attempted to obtain commissions and performances for their works, but the San Diego area was not as active artistically as Chicago. Despite their happiness in being with one another, they were interested in locating a more sophisticated environment in which to produce their works. When Miss Britain's Suite for Strings [W16] (1940) was awarded the First National Prize sponsored by the Sigma Alpha Iota National Sorority, she planned to combine a trip with her husband to receive the award in Los Angeles with an exploration of that city, Santa Barbara, and San Francisco. Of the three, Los Angeles seemed the most appropriate to them. In 1941 they moved there, purchasing an Italian-style home in the Hollywood Hills. Their home, which they christened *Casa del Sogno* (house of our dream), became a setting for the display and creation of their respective works.

In Los Angeles Miss Britain found ample composition and piano students and Simone found employment at the movie studios. They became active in the social circles of Hollywood, mingling with local and international personalities. Miss Britain's recent works, frequently winning prizes and awards around the country, were performed by ensembles throughout the United States. After discovering a remarkable similarity between her own metaphysical beliefs and those expressed in Ernest Holmes' book *The Science of Mind*, Miss Britain became a devotee of Ernest Holmes and attended many of his services.[3] The *Science of Mind* magazine remains a daily source of inspirational comfort for Miss Britain.

The next ten years of Miss Britain's life were very creative, resulting in new works inspired by new situations and experiences. Trips to Mexico with Simone and a general fascination for Latin rhythms led to *Serenata Sorrentina* for small orchestra [W23] (1946) and the later creation of piano pieces such as *Torillo* [W104] (1949) and *Ensenada* [W115] (1956). A visit to a friend's home in Crestline, a town in the San Bernardino mountains of southern California, resulted in *We Believe* for orchestra [W20] (1942). The *Jewels of Lake Tahoe* for orchestra [W21] (1945) had its origins in a camping vacation at the famous mountain lake, and *Umpqua Forest* for orchestra [W24] (1946) was born on a visit to an Oregon fishing camp. The orchestral works *Red Clay* [W22] (1946) and *Paint Horse and Saddle* [W25] (1947) were inspired by visits to Amarillo and reflections of her pioneer background. They join the earlier *Drouth* [W11] (1939), *Canyon* [W10] (1939), and the later *Chicken in the Rough* [W26] (1951), *Cactus Rhapsody* [W27] (1953), and the *Cowboy Rhapsody* [W30] (1956) in defining a "Western" emphasis, complete with quotations of cowboy songs and Indian rhythms, for this period of her development. In addition, the 1940s produced works such as the *Phantasy* for oboe and orchestra [W19] (1942) and numerous songs, many of them composed to texts by Miss Britain's friends.

In 1949 Edgardo Simone suffered a stroke which greatly diminished his creative powers. Later that year he died of complications related to the stroke. Miss Britain, although heartbroken, found strength in her metaphysical beliefs, which stressed a sense of oneness with nature that transcended life and death. As always, she continued to seek spiritual enlightenment through her art.

Despite the setback in her personal life, the 1950s were productive for Miss Britain. On the pedagogical side of her career came the publication *How To Play The Piano* [W105] and a number of piano pieces for students. Miss Britain received an honorary doctorate from the Amarillo Musical Arts Conservatory (June 1958), and her works, including the *Cowboy Rhapsody* [W30], were played by the Amarillo Symphony. One of her larger projects of the decade was the three-act opera *Carillon* [W155] (1952), composed in collaboration with the noted author Rupert Hughes. Although Miss Britain and Hughes had hoped that it would be performed by the Metropolitan Opera, it was never produced.

Miss Britain's music continued to find new interpreters in the 1950s. Colonel George Howard, conductor of the United States Air Force Symphony Orchestra, gave extensive exposure to works such as *Saturnale*, *Prelude to a Drama*, and *Prison* in domestic and foreign performances. On a tour of Europe with her daughter Lerae, *Drouth* [W11] (1939) was performed in Madrid by Vincente Spiteri and the Madrid Symphony Orchestra (1960).

In the 1950s, Miss Britain also increased her level of activity in the National League of American Pen Women, a group she had joined while she lived in Chicago. The 1957 premiere of *Saturnale* (1939) by the United States Air Force Symphony Orchestra, at the National Convention of the American Pen Women in Washington, D.C., marked an award of honor bestowed upon her by the group.

In 1955 Miss Britain met Theodore Morton, a pioneer aviator, who rekindled her desire for a romantic life. Soon Miss Britain came to the conclusion that great love, or great tragedy, inspired a composer to find stronger melodies. They were married in December of 1959, and Morton, although not a musician, has remained supportive of Miss Britain's career to the present day.

The years since 1960 have been marked by steady streams of new works, awards, and performances. The *Prelude to a Drama* was performed in Moscow by Konstantin Ivanov and the Moscow Symphony Orchestra (1961). The Brentwood-Westwood Symphony, a community orchestra active in West Los Angeles, performed many of Miss Britain's works under the direction of conductor Alvin Mills. Other community orchestras in the Los Angeles area, such as the Whittier, Glendale, Highland Park, Wilshire, and Downey Symphonies, featured Miss Britain's works on their programs. Individual works have also been performed by ensembles throughout the United States and Europe. Recent festivals of music by women composers have included a number of Miss Britain's pieces.

Nisan [W187], a work for chorus and orchestra on a text by Kate Hammond, won first prize in an international contest sponsored by Delta Omicron International Fraternity, and it was premiered under their sponsorship by the Detroit Symphony in 1961. Marygrove College in Detroit commissioned *The Dark Lady Within* [W158] (1962), a ballet based on Shakespearean sonnets, and *The Flute Song* [W194] (1965) for female choir. The National Society of Arts and Letters produced Miss Britain's chamber opera *Kuthara* [W157] (1960) in Santa Barbara as a benefit for their organization. *Western Testament* [W160] (1964), another ballet, was commissioned by St. Mary's College in Omaha, Nebraska. *Cosmic Mist Symphony* [W33] (1962) was awarded the first national prize in a contest sponsored by the National League of American Pen Women. It was performed in an open rehearsal by the Houston Symphony Orchestra under the direction of A. Clyde Roller in 1967 as part of a symposium on contemporary music.

Of a number of countries visited with her husband on a trip to the Mediterranean, the sights of Egypt inspired an *Egyptian Suite* [W123] (1969) for piano, from which *The Pyramids of Giza* [W148, W37] was arranged for organ and for small orchestra. A symposium on modern composition inspired her to compose a twelve-tone piece, *Les Fameux Douze (The Famous Twelve)* [W36](1965) for orchestra. Although she was not pleased with the work, it won a prize from the National League of American Pen Women. A trip to Alaska inspired the *Alaskan Trail of '98* [W122] (1967) for piano (also for orchestra, W38), which memorializes the pioneers of the Alaskan gold rush. Among her latest orchestral works are *Anwar Sadat (In Memory)* [W39] (1982), *Earth of God* [W40] (1984), *Sam Houston* [W41] (1987), and *Texas* [W42] (1987).

Miss Britain's activities since 1960 have included the duties of music editor for *The Penwomen* magazine, and a selection of her articles from that magazine have been published in book form as *Composer's Corner*.[4] These articles explore issues of creativity and the creative process, philosophy, and practical musical concerns. Recurring topics include nationalism and women in music. Throughout the volume Miss Britain refers to statements made by great musicians and other great thinkers to support and amplify her own ideas. Miss Britain has also written an autobiography, which she soon hopes to see published, and an unpublished autobiographical novel, "Bravo." Discussions of her life and works have been included in Madeline Goss's *Modern Music Makers*[5] and in Jane Weiner LePage's *Selected Biographies of Women Composers, Conductors, and Musicians of the Twentieth Century*.[6]

Recent tributes to Miss Britain are numerous. She was honored by the region of her birth at the opening of the Square House Museum in Panhandle, Texas. She has also received awards from the Mary Carr Moore Manuscript Society. The late Hans Moldenhauer acquired some of her original manuscripts for his archives. Many of her orchestral scores are housed in the Edwin A. Fleischer Collection in Philadelphia, which serves as a permanent repository, open to conductors, for such materials. Miss Britain's daughter, Lerae Britain, recently retired from a career in education, has expressed an interest in promoting her mother's music.

Miss Britain is a member of ASCAP, International Committee for Los Angeles Philharmonic Orchestra, American Music Center (New York), National Association for American Composers and Conductors (Washington, D.C.), Los Angeles World Affairs Council, National Association for American Composers and Conductors (Los Angeles), Woman's Chamber Music Society, National League of American Penwomen, Brentwood Symphony Woman's Guild, MacDowell Colony Association, Texas Composers Forum, International League of Women Composers, American Music Composers, and Around the World Club. She is an honorary member of Sigma Alpha

Iota National Musical Sorority, Federation of Music Clubs of Texas, Etude Music Club of Los Angeles, Philharmonic Club of Amarillo, Schubert Club of Los Angeles, Texas Music Teachers Association, MacDowell Club of Amarillo, Harmony Club of Amarillo, Dominant Club of Los Angeles, and the National Institute of Fine Arts of Beverly Hills, California. She is listed in Who's Who in America, Who's Who in Music, Who's Who in American Women, and the Royal Blue Book of England.

Miss Britain continues to compose, motivated and invigorated by her optimistic outlook on life and her metaphysical philosophies. Her most recent works demonstrate a continued identification with Texas, the region of her birth, and she makes no attempt to hide her disdain for avant-garde trends in music. For Miss Britain, melody is paramount. "My ambition has been to search deeply for an inspired melody from the heart," she writes, "with strength and purpose over a compatible harmonic background. Then I feel free to move into contemporary fields, atonally, if desired, but with a rhythmic pulse that is interesting and exciting, which can grow out of the theme. Hopefully, when the composition is recalled, its character and essence is immediately recognized."[7] From her debut in Munich to the present day her melodic works have delighted performers and audiences alike.

Notes

1. The authors are indebted to Radie Britain, to her collection of clippings, and to her unpublished "Autobiography: Ridin' Herd to Writing Symphonies" for background and biographical information and for information on the development of her personal and musical philosophies. Important dates have been verified through contemporary periodicals and newspapers and through public records in Amarillo. A. G. Mojtabai's *Blessèd Assurance* (Boston: Houghton Mifflin, 1986) provided a brief general history of the panhandle region.

2. The Methodist college closed in 1927 and the buildings were donated to the city of Clarendon. Clarendon College operates today as a public junior college.

3. Ernest Holmes, *The Science of Mind: A Complete Course of Lessons in the Science of Mind and Spirit* (New York: R.M. McBride and Company, 1926 [and later revised and enlarged editions]).

4. Hollywood: Highland Music Company, 1978.

5. New York: E.P. Dutton, 1952.

6. Metuchen, N. J.: Scarecrow Press, 1980.

7. *Composer's Corner*, page 4.

Interview: December 1988

When did you first become interested in composing?

I took my first compositions, several short pieces, to Europe with me and played them for my future instructor, Dr. Noelte. My daughter asked me the other day, "What were the names of the pieces?" and I said, "Well, one of them was *Ocean Moods* [W81]." Here I was living on the prairies of Texas and I'm crazy about the ocean!

Dr. Noelte found my first compositions so interesting that he said he'd like to take me as his protégé. So that was my big break.

Had you had any instruction in composition before that?

Oh, yes, I did creative work when I studied counterpoint in Chicago with Arthur Olaf Andersen as part of the requirements for my degree in piano performance. But when I went to Europe I had decided not to become a concert pianist. I'd worked all my life to be a pianist, but I wanted to create. I was so afraid my parents would be disappointed that I'd changed my mind. My mother wrote back and she said, "Anyone can be a pianist, it takes someone special to become a composer." I was so relieved, after they spent so much money on me to become a pianist.

Had anyone seen your compositions before?

No, I'd never shown them to anyone. I never thought they were anything out of the ordinary—I wasn't happy with the fundamentals that I'd received at the American Conservatory and at Clarendon College. I felt awfully weak in harmony and counterpoint even after I'd gotten my diploma. I explained this to Dr. Noelte and I think he was impressed by my honesty. He said, "I'll instruct you; we'll have a lesson every day. We'll go through harmony like lightning because I know how to simplify it." Later, when I began to teach counterpoint, I realized how important it was to see that my pupils understood, step by step, the rules of harmony because if you don't, you will never master it.

Did you compose your early pieces shortly before you went to Germany or had you written them a long time before your departure?

No, I didn't write them specially to take to Germany. I was in Texas teaching when I wrote them.

When I started [lessons with Dr. Noelte], I wanted to begin composing immediately. He gave me a poem by Robert Burns and told me to write just the introduction. When I showed him my work, he said, "Have you ever heard Wagner's *Siegfried?*" In fact, I hadn't heard any Wagnerian operas. He gets a score, and shows me an identical theme to what I had written. And I had never heard it! He looked at me and shook his head in amazement.

But he wasn't happy with the introduction to that poem. So one day he suggested that I go into the woods and spend the day in meditation with nature. That was a great lesson for me to be alone and feel the power of something greater than I was that was all around us and in us.

Before you studied with Dr. Noelte, what kind of music influenced you? What kind of music did you want to write as a composer?

I don't think I had given that too much thought.

What influence did Dr. Noelte have upon you?

I had gone up to Berlin first but my instructor didn't speak any English and I was just stymied trying to work under those conditions. When I got down to Munich, Dr. Noelte spoke better English than I did!

As I said before, I had never heard Wagner. To show you how careful he was in training me, he said, "You go up to Oberammergau and spend a weekend. I'm going to give you a book on Wagner. You stay up there and devour it in those Bavarian Alps." What a revelation that was. When I heard Wagner performed by the Munich Opera Company, I could hardly sit in my seat, I was so moved!

That's the greatest thing that ever happened to me—to have found Dr. Noelte. I look back now and think how different my life would have been if I hadn't found such a great scholar. He was a friend of Richard Strauss. I'd go with him every evening to concerts because he was a critic. I knew how I had been impressed [by the performance] and then I'd read in the newspaper the next morning how he was impressed. You can imagine what a lesson it was.

The artists would come to a cafe and we'd have supper together and I'd listen to their comments. "Why didn't you take your hand down at one place?" and all these little nuances. It was a revelation to me.

I spent two years over there and then lost my sister. I was so upset. I was afraid I wouldn't be able to study with him any more. He believed in my talent enought that he said, "If you can't come back, I'll come to Chicago because I promised that I'd put you on your feet and make you an independent composer." He lived up to it. Those things happen once in a lifetime.

You've written so many pieces for orchestra.

Orchestra is my great love. I never get as much satisfaction out of writing for piano or violin. It doesn't fulfill what I'm searching for. I love the color and the way you can make your melody fit like a glove with the instruments. Of course you've got to know how to orchestrate. One time I wrote a piece and I think I went one note higher than was possible for the flute and Dr. Noelte had a little "ha-ha" written over the part. So you have to watch very carefully.

When you were first starting to compose, what kind of preparation did you make before you wrote something for orchestra?

I jumped in there real fast. I kept telling Dr. Noelte, "I want to write for orchestra." He said, "We'll begin scoring for four horns. If you can score well for four horns, like a hymn, you'll at least have a good backbone and your music won't be thin and sound like it's going to fall apart." And I remember that was my first exercise in orchestral technique. My first orchestral composition was an *Intermezzo* [*Symphonic Intermezzo*, W2]. I received good notices when it was performed.

Of course, my organ training was also beneficial. I had studied organ at that girls' school [Crescent College]. If you have a melody, does it fit the pipes for the clarinet, or the oboe, and all that business. But I seemed to hear that when I was scoring. You know, which instrument should play a melody? I'm sure it was the organ that helped me a great deal.

You had studied orchestration in the conservatory?

Oh, I studied orchestration but I really didn't learn much. I scored Beethoven and Schubert and Brahms symphonies. I just didn't get a good foundation.

But Dr. Noelte rarely changed my orchestration. I can't remember him rejecting anything that I was creating. I think Richard Strauss influenced me, because Dr. Noelte was so impressed by his orchestration, as well as Ravel. Just so gorgeous.

What kinds of preparations do you make to compose?

You first must live with an idea. I get a title, I believe, first, and put it on the back burner and let it set awhile. I'm very spiritual when it comes to composing. I tune in to something greater than I am, I feel that I am the reed through which the melody is played. It's never let me down. If I can dismiss all vibrations of this earth and be really quiet, I begin to hear a beautiful melody. And I begin writing it down as fast as I can.

It has made me very spiritual because I believe that God is everywhere. He's in you, He's all around you, and all you have to do is to tune in and here He is. It's just unbelievable what any of us can do when we work with the force! I seem to have caught on to that. I bow my head at the piano and quietly listen and it's just unbelievable. It's been a beautiful, inspiring experience, to know that the force is there. I'm not so sure but music is God. Where all this comes from, I just can't comprehend. All I do is to tune in and, afterwards, I think, "Oh, thank you God, it's so gorgeous."

That's why I've never gotten egotistical about composing because I am only the medium through which it comes. I believe many artists work that way. I gave a talk last week to some poets and painters and I'm sure that it's the same principal for all creators.

When the idea comes to you, is it just a melody or are there harmonies along with it?

Mostly melody. When I begin listening carefully I put harmony with it. Like *Epiphyllum* [W120]. I didn't have that worked out at all. But it just flowed, it just kept on. The greatest thing that happens to a composer is to keep a melodic line extended and not just write a few measures and then go to something else. Like *Prison* [W47]. It doesn't stop, it's just one continuous line. I wrote that in two hours. I was inspired and I just kept on and on and on until the composition was finished.

Another thing that's so important in composing is to develop all the technique that is possible. You can hear these melodies but if you can't do anything with them, what is it worth? You've got to reverse them and juggle them all over. Especially in orchestration. Extending your thoughts is also helped by knowing counterpoint and harmony. Tchaikovsky said it was always difficult for him to make a bridge going from one idea to another. Now that should be just as inspired as what you've been working with for a main theme. But that takes brainwork and patience.

When you think of all the pieces that you've written, do you group them together in any way? Do you think of style periods, such as the early part of your career or the middle part of your career or a Chicago portion or a Texas portion?

No, I don't think so.

But have there been changes in your style from year to year?

I should tell you that when I wrote the *Saturnale* [W14] they rehearsed it with the Chicago Symphony and Dr. Noelte nearly had a fit. He said that I was writing "Latin music." He said, "That's not the way I trained you." Well, I wanted to get it out of my system and I don't think that it hurt me. But he didn't like it. He said, "That's not the kind of work that you're going to do."

After you wrote *Saturnale* did you....

No, I never did do anything like that again.

It was just a temporary change of style?

Yes. I'm sure it was on account of meeting this Italian [Edgardo Simone]. He insisted on me writing that "from the heart."

Have there been other changes?

I think I started reaching out more in the modern idiom when I started composing pieces about outer space. Like the *Cosmic Mist Symphony* [W33]. I think I changed my style quite a bit to try to catch that mood. I've written quite a few other works concerning outer space.

How are those works different than the others?

Well I think they're more modern, I guess you would say, more contemporary. Outer space is so mysterious; we know so little about it. It draws on your fantasy more. You can't be earthbound when you're writing about the stars. I've got one movement titled *Spacewalk* [*Translunar Cycle,* W265, W77]; I was so enraptured when the astronauts first landed on the moon that it just sent me. I've done a lot of research on outer space.

How would you describe the difference in musical terms?

I think it's a little bit more impressionistic.

Were there any other stylistic changes?

I wrote one piece [*Les Fameux Douze (The Famous Twelve),* W36] in the twelve-tone manner, like Schoenberg, and I hated it. But I thought, "Well, it's an experiment, I'm going to see if I can do it." I wrote it for small orchestra and then put it in a contest and it won $250. But I have never shown it to a conductor. I just wanted to see if I could do it for the technical experience.

You cannot write a piece and have it be a brain tumor, you might say. You've got to have your soul and your heart mixed up with it, I think. I don't want to write cerebral music—there's too much of it written today. After hearing some far-out music you think, "Thank God that's over, I hope I never have to hear that again." But I don't think that it will last. Composers are beginning to write music that the audience will enjoy also. You can't force people with that kind of music [cerebral music], I don't think. There's something about it that is unreal.

Is *The Famous Twelve* the "wildest" piece that you've written?

Yes, and it's the worst!

Have you done any other experiments like that?

No, I don't think so. I didn't see any particular reason. Of course, if you play my pieces for average people, they think they're very modern. Dr. Stock of the Chicago Symphony once told me when he finished rehearsing *Prelude to a Drama* [W1]; "You must think of your audience when you're writing, not just yourself."

What plans do you have for future compositions?

I've got two or three good titles for mood pictures, to catch different moods, like *Surf and Sand* [W133]. That's for piano. It's rather modern, too. One I want to do is called "Illumination." I want to do something with that title just to see what happens.

You frequently start with a title. What does the title do for you?

I think that it sets the tone of the spirit that I desire. Like this little piece called *Upbeat* [W136]. It just hits you, like a flash. It's more "popular" than most of the things that I write. I usually don't feel popular music but I like the rhythm. I'm looking to be inspired.

I wrote to Nancy Reagan to complain that she kept putting on all these nightclub acts, like Liza Minnelli, in the White House. I said, "Let's get out of the nightclub when we're in the White House. You've got a great orchestra right there in Washington, draw on it and bring those musicians in and give us an inspired evening."

I've already written to Mrs. Bush, because her husband said that what he really enjoyed was folk songs from Tennessee. I told her, "Have Rostropovich's opinion. He will be so happy to work with you and he's got so many great artists that I'm sure he can build beautiful programs for you."

Have you used folk tunes in your music?

Oh, yes, I've done a lot of cowboy songs. I've done quite a few Western ones—*Western Suite* ("Covered Wagon," "Stampede") [W83], *Ridin' Herd in Texas* [W121], *Cowboy Rhapsody* [W30], *Cactus Rhapsody* [W109]. [Nikolai] Sokoloff told me when he heard my compositions, "Get over your own soil and write. Keep that folk tune going." But I think I've almost exhausted it. There's a limit to how many cowboy songs or Indian rhythms you can do. In one piece, *Red Clay* [W22], I used a lot of Indian rhythms.

Who are the twentieth century composers that you admire?

Of course I like Shostakovich very much—I think he's a great composer. Copland is very clever and he's taken some of our folk tunes and done some very nice things. And John Adams, he's got a certain something that's different. It's something to be reckoned with, it's original, I think.

I never was crazy about Gershwin; I think that *Rhapsody in Blue* has a terrific melody, beautiful, but it hurts me when they say that he's the greatest American composer. But he's got that reputation.

One of the big issues of your career has been how being a woman has influenced what you've accomplished.

Well, that's been difficult. Very difficult. It's still difficult. And I'll tell you where our big problem is: you need to know conductors on a friendly basis. The minute a woman gets started to become more friendly, the conductor's wives think, as a rule, that you're trying to flirt with them. And you can't invite them over for lunch and sit around and talk to them about your work. But a man can. Two men can get together easier. I remember when I wanted Wallenstein to do *Prelude to a Drama* [W1], I'd keep going backstage and his wife would be holding his arm all the time I was talking to him. I guess he was a ladies' man! I'd have that to fight!

You need to hobknob around with these conductors. I'd like to know Andre Previn [the former conductor of the Los Angeles Philharmonic] real well. He knew me the minute I went backstage—"Oh yeah, Radie Britain, I know you"—because I knew his father. But you need to become buddy-buddy with them, just like I am with Colonel [George] Howard [of the United States Air Force Symphony Orchestra]. He would do any piece that I'd write, he believes in me and knows me. But if they don't know you, they've got many other composers that they do know and admire.

That's been difficult. You've got to keep your place as a lady and not try to influence them unfairly. Somebody once accused me of passing a $100 bill to get a performance. I'd never do that, I wouldn't think of that, I don't think that I'd get a performance. But you can't let it bother you. My teacher told me that it's no bed of roses but if I could walk on the thorns I'd make it. So I just keep walking on the thorns.

My name's good because they can't tell whether I'm a man or a woman. Howard Hanson, you see, didn't know I was a woman. But, even my looks are against me being a serious composer! They brought some movie people in here one day and they said, "I want you to look at her. Can you imagine her writing serious music? She ought to be writing popular stuff." You just take what you have, you can't change it.

You can get your music in their hands and stay away from them so they don't have to look at you. I remember once I wanted a conductor to look at my work and I'm sure he looked at me and thought, "She probably writes little old dinky stuff." I said, "Just look at one of my pieces." "Well, come over during rehearsal, during intermission and I'll look at a score." And I remember he took it and he started saying, "Well, very good, very good" and then "Damn good!" But you see, they don't expect it.

When my teacher was trying to get my pieces published, they refused him several times and he kept going back, going back. "She's got something to say." "Well, all right" and, finally, they published it. That helped me a great deal. But he could open doors for me. He opened the door for my performances in Chicago with the Chicago Symphony. He kept having coffee with this conductor. I guess to get rid of him he said, "Well, I'll play it."

I don't bemoan it. I think it's marvelous to be a woman. I love the combination of male and female. It's a terrific combination.

What has been the most fruitful part of your career? When did you feel the best about what you were writing and about the performances that your works were receiving?

The most fruitful time was when Harry Seitz premiered my *Nisan* [W187; with the Detroit Symphony Orchestra and Chorus in 1961]. That was the highest I ever got. I thought, "I'm finally on top." They just clapped and clapped—a standing ovation. You don't get that very often. They just kept clapping. I took my third bow and looked over at Dr. Seitz and he was flat on the floor. I thought, "Oh, my Lord, he's dead!" He wasn't, as it turned out. And the policemen came, "Empty the hall, empty the hall." I couldn't even talk to the people that liked the work so well. Later, I asked Dr. Seitz what happened and he replied, "Your music was so beautiful that it overwhelmed me!" And I thought, "You just don't make it to the top. You don't ever quite get there."

How would you describe yourself?

I'm a worker, I think that's the best thing I have to offer. I don't care what price I have to pay; I'd stay up all night until I learned something. And I've got determination, always have. I hate to waste time, it just breaks me up to lose a lot of time, because that's the greatest thing we have.

When *Saturnale* [W14] was played back in Washington they gave me a standing ovation. But I don't get too vain over it. There's just so darn much more to learn. I don't live in the past too much. I remember telling my teacher once that I felt so ignorant on so many subjects. He said, "You can't learn everything well. Do one well and be contented with that." But I like to learn about a lot of things, branch out a little.

I think life is just a terrific challenge. But my life has been very exciting, to tell you the truth. And I've enjoyed most of it. I've met so many interesting people. When I was a little girl I always wanted to edge up to bankers and lawyers and ask them all kinds of questions. I've always wanted to get with someone who knew more than I knew and bleed their brains. Now I just read and read like mad. I'm a ferocious reader of biographies about great people.

If you had to describe your music to someone, say a conductor, and you couldn't play a tape for them right then, how would you describe it?

Well, I'd say, "If you want real good, juicy melodies, something from the heart that the orchestra likes to play and the audience enjoys, you might enjoy my work." It isn't cerebral music at all.

Works and Performances

ORCHESTRA AND BAND

W1. *Prelude To A Drama* (1928) Chicago

3-2-2-2, 4-3-3-1, timp., perc., strings. 6 minutes.

Published as Overture to *Pygmalion* by Seesaw Music Corporation. Score and parts also available from the Fleisher Collection. Additional copies of the score available from the American Heritage Center (University of Wyoming); Library of Congress; UCLA Music Library.

Originally titled Overture to Pygmalion. *Title changed at conductor's request for performance during Holy Week (see W1b).*

PREMIERE

W1a. 1937 (January 31); Chicago; Illinois Symphony Orchestra; Albert Goldberg, conductor. *See:* B70, 71, 72, 73.

OTHER SELECTED PERFORMANCES

W1b. 1938 (April 14, 15); Chicago; Chicago Symphony Orchestra; Dr. Frederick Stock, conductor. *See:* B77, 78, 79, 80, 81, 82, 85.

W1c. 1938 (July 25); Chicago; Chicago Philharmonic Orchestra; Richard Czerwonky, conductor.

W1d. 1939 (October 26); Rochester, New York; Rochester Symphony Orchestra; Dr. Howard Hanson, conductor.

W1e. 1942 (January 21); Los Angeles; WPA Los Angeles Symphony; James Sample, conductor. *See:* B97, 98, 99.

W1f. 1949 (October 9); Burbank, California; Burbank Symphony Orchestra; Leo Damani, conductor.

W1g. 1950 (February 16, 17); Los Angeles; Los Angeles Philharmonic Orchestra; Alfred Wallenstein, conductor. *See:* B109, 110, 111, 112.

W1h. 1952 (November 18); Atlanta; Atlanta Symphony Orchestra; Henry Sopkin, conductor.

W1i. 1952 (November 19); Gainsville, Georgia; Atlanta Symphony Orchestra; Henry Sopkin, conductor.

W1j. 1955 (February 13); Washington, D.C.; United States Air Force Symphony Orchestra; Colonel George Howard, conductor.

W1k. 1955 (April 13); tape recording broadcast in Cairo, Egypt; United States Air Force Symphony; Colonel George Howard, conductor. *See:* B116, 117.

W1l. 1955 (April 15); tape recording broadcast on ABC National Network; United States Air Force Symphony Orchestra; Colonel George Howard, conductor. *See:* B116, 117.

W1m. 1955 (June 10); Trondheim (formerly Nidaros), Norway; United States Air Force Symphony Orchestra; Colonel George Howard, conductor. *See:* B116, 117.

W1n. 1955 (June 29); Wiesbaden, Germany; United States Air Force Symphony Orchestra; Colonel George Howard, conductor. *See:* B116, 117.

W1o. 1955 (July 1); Frankfurt, Germany; United States Air Force Symphony Orchestra; Colonel George Howard, conductor. *See:* B116, 117.

W1p. 1956 (March 1); KHG Western and Hawaii; United States Air Force Symphony Orchestra; Colonel George Howard, conductor.

W1q. 1956 (November 20); Oakland, California; Oakland Symphony Orchestra; Orley See, conductor.

W1r. 1959 (January 27); Amarillo, Texas; Amarillo Symphony Orchestra; A. Clyde Roller, conductor.

W1s. 1959 (May 7); Washington, D.C.; United States Air Force Symphony Orchestra; Col. George Howard, conductor.

W1t. 1961 (August 11); Moscow; Moscow Symphony Orchestra; Konstantin Ivanov, conductor. *See:* B125.

W1u. 1964 (January 6); Chicago; Northside Symphony Orchestra; Milton Preeves, conductor.

W1v. 1965 (January 24); Los Angeles; Hollywood-Wilshire Symphony Orchestra; Victor DePinto, conductor.

W1w. 1969 (April 19); Thousand Oaks, California; Thousand Oaks Symphony Orchestra; Elmer Ramsey, conductor.

W1x. 1970 (December 13); Pasadena, California; Highland Park Symphony Orchestra; Frank Desby, conductor.

W1y. 1971 (November 5); Los Angeles; Highland Park Symphony Orchestra; Frank Desby, conductor.

W1z. 1972 (December 3); Los Angeles; Brentwood-Westwood Symphony Orchestra; Alvin Mills, conductor.

W1aa. 1974 (March 9); Downey, California; Downey Symphony.

W1bb. 1979 (June 3); Los Angeles; Los Angeles Council of Music and Arts for Senior Citizens' Symphony Orchestra; Louis Palange, conductor.

W2. *Symphonic Intermezzo* (1928) Chicago

3-2-2-2, 4-3-3-1, timp., perc., and strings. 7 minutes.

Unpublished; score and parts available from Heroico Music Publications.

PREMIERE

W2a. 1928 (January 8); Chicago; Chicago Woman's Symphony; Ethel Leginska, conductor. *See:* B42, 43, 45, 46, 47, 48, 50.

OTHER SELECTED PERFORMANCES

W2b. 1928 (February 18); Somerville, Massachusetts; Boston Woman's Symphony Orchestra; Ethel Leginska, conductor. *See:* B52.

W2c. 1928 (February 19); Boston; Boston Woman's Symphony Orchestra; Ethel Leginska, conductor.

w2d. 1928 (August 2); Conneaut Lake, Pennsylvania; Boston Woman's Symphony Orchestra; Ethel Leginska, conductor.

W3. *Heroic Poem* (1929) Chicago

3-2-2-2, 4-3-3-1, timp., perc., strings. 8 minutes.

Published for the Juilliard School by the American Music Center, 1946. Score and parts also available from the Fleisher Collection. Additional copies of the score available from the Boston Public Library; New York Public Library; UCLA Music Library.

Juilliard National Publication Prize 1930.
Hollywood Bowl Prize 1930. *See:* B53, 118.

Dedicated to Colonel Charles Lindbergh's flight to Paris.

PREMIERE

W3a. 1932 (March 3); Rochester, New York; Rochester Philharmonic Orchestra; Dr. Howard Hanson, conductor.

OTHER SELECTED PERFORMANCES

W3b. 1933 (July 6); Chicago; Chicago Philharmonic Orchestra; Richard Czerwonky, conductor. *See:* B54, 55, 56, 57, 58, 59, 60, 61, 62, 63.

W3c. 1934 (October 9); Chicago; Woman's Symphony Orchestra; Ebba Sundstrom, conductor.

W3d. 1936 (July 27); Chicago; Chicago Philharmonic Orchestra; Richard Czerwonky, conductor.

W3e. 1937 (September 4); Chicago; Chicago Philharmonic Orchestra; Richard Czerwonky, conductor.

W3f. 1937 (December 20); New York; WPA Orchestra; Edgar Schenkman, conductor.

W3g. 1956 (March 11); Atlanta; Atlanta Symphony Orchestra; Henry Sopkin, conductor. *See:* B118.

W4. *Rhapsodic Phantasie* for Piano and Orchestra (1933) Chicago

2-2-2-2, 3-3-3-1, timp., perc., strings. 16 minutes.

Unpublished; score and parts available from Heroico Music Publications.

First State Prize, Texas Federation of Music Clubs, 1939.
First National Prize, National League of American Pen Women, 1945.

PREMIERE

W4a. 1938 (April 24); Chicago; Illinois Symphony Orchestra; Izler Solomon, conductor; Rose Goldberg, soloist. *See:* B83, 84, 86.

OTHER SELECTED PERFORMANCES

W4b. 1946 (October 13); Los Angeles; Los Angeles Symphony Orchestra; Ethel Leginska, conductor; Lyle Kennedy, soloist.

W4c. 1948 (January 18); Los Angeles; Leginska Symphony Orchestra; Ethel Leginska, conductor; Lyle Kennedy, soloist.

W5. *Nocturn* for Small Orchestra (1934) Chicago

2-2-2-1, 2-2-2-0, timp., perc., strings. 8 minutes.

Unpublished; score and parts available from the Fleisher Collection.

PREMIERE

W5a. 1940 (November 10); Chicago; Woman's Concert Ensemble; Fanny Arnsten Hassler, conductor.

OTHER SELECTED PERFORMANCES

W5b. 1946 (January 19); Hollywood, California; Studio orchestra broadcast on KFI radio; Claude Sweeten, conductor.

W5c. 1948 (April 3); Atlanta; Atlanta Symphony Orchestra; Henry Sopkin, conductor. *See:* B106.

W5d. 1948 (April 7); Atlanta; Atlanta Symphony Orchestra; Henry Sopkin, conductor. *See:* B107.

W5e. 1949 (March 28); Atlanta; Atlanta Symphony Orchestra; Henry Sopkin, conductor.

W5f. 1954 (September 29); Mexico City; Mexico Chamber Symphony; Louis Herria de la Fuenta, conductor.

W5g. 1955 (February 22); Amarillo, Texas; Amarillo Symphony Orchestra; A. Clyde Roller, conductor. *See:* B114, 115.

w5h. 1985 (December 1); Los Angeles; Brentwood-Westwood Symphony Orchestra; Alvin Mills, conductor.

w5i. 1986 (March 22); Atlanta; Sandy Springs Chamber Orchestra; David MacKenzie, conductor. In conjunction with the Fourth International Congress on Women in Music at the School of Music, Georgia State University.

w5j. 1988 (March 9); Dallas, Texas; Southern Methodist University Orchestra; Anshel Brusilow, conductor.

W6. *Infant Suite* **(The Infant, Berceuse, Toy Parade)** (1935) MacDowell Colony, Peterborough, New Hampshire

1-1-1-1, 1-1-0-0, timp., perc., strings. 7 minutes.

Unpublished; score and parts available from the Fleisher Collection.

Originally for solo piano (*see:* W85).

Dedicated to Lerae Britain, the composer's daughter.

PREMIERE

w6a. 1936 (February 14); Los Angeles; WPA Symphony Orchestra; Modest Altschuler, conductor.

OTHER SELECTED PERFORMANCES

w6b. 1937 (March 16); New York; New York ensemble broadcast on WGN radio. Alfred Wallenstein, conductor. *See:* B74.

w6c. 1937 (April 15); New York; New York ensemble broadcast on WOR radio; Alfred Wallenstein, conductor. *See:* B74.

w6d. 1937 (December 18); Chicago; Philharmonic Woman's Symphony; Fanny Arnsten-Hassler, conductor. *See:* B75.

w6e. 1938 (February 13); Chicago; Illinois Symphony Orchestra; Albert Goldberg, conductor. *See:* B76.

w6f. 1939 (January 27); Amarillo, Texas; Amarillo Symphony Orchestra; Murry Meeker, conductor.

w6g. 1941 (January 16); Amarillo, Texas; Amarillo Symphony Orchestra; Robert Barron, conductor.

W7. *Light* (1935) MacDowell Colony, Peterborough, New Hampshire

3-3-3-3, 4-3-3-1, timp., perc., strings. 8 minutes.

Unpublished; score and parts available from the Fleisher Collection.

First National Prize, Boston Woman's Symphony Orchestra, 1941.
See: B94.
First National Prize, National League of American Pen Women, 1985.

Dedicated to Thomas Edison.

PREMIERE

W7a. 1938 (November 29); Chicago; Chicago Woman's Symphony Orchestra; Gladys Welge, conductor. *See:* B87, 88.

OTHER SELECTED PERFORMANCES

W7b. 1941 (May 25); Boston; Boston Woman's Symphony Orchestra; Alexander Thiede, conductor. *See:* B94.

W7c. 1990 (March 4); Brentwood, California; Brentwood-Westwood Symphony Orchestra; Alvin Mills, conductor.

W8. *Prison (Lament)* for Russian instruments (1935) Chicago

Unpublished; location of score unknown.

Originally for violin and piano (*see:* W47).

W9. *Southern Symphony* (Maestoso Allegro, Adagio, Rhumbando, Allegro) (1935) MacDowell Colony, Peterborough, New Hampshire

3-3-3-3, 4-3-3-1, timp., perc., strings. 23 minutes.

Unpublished; score and parts available from the Fleisher Collection. Additional copies of the score for "Rhumbando" available from the Library of Congress; UCLA Music Library. Original pencil sketch of opening page included in the Moldenhauer Collection, Harvard University.

Second movement dedicated to Edgar Charles Britain.

W9a. 1940 (March 4); Chicago; Illinois Symphony Orchestra; Izler Solomon, conductor. *See:* B91, 92.

OTHER SELECTED PERFORMANCES

W9b. "Rhumbando": 1940 (June 24); Chicago; Philharmonic Orchestra; Richard Czerwonky, conductor.

W9c. 1961 (June 13); Washington, D.C.; United States Air Force Symphony; Colonel George Howard, conductor.

In Living Ecstasy [voice and orchestra] 1938. *See:* W225.

Sunken City [voice and orchestra] 1938. *See:* W226.

Twilight Moon [voice and orchestra] 1938. *See:* W228.

Open The Door To Me [voice and orchestra] 1939. *See:* W229.

W10. *Canyon* (1939) Chicago

3-3-3-3, 4-3-3-1, timp., perc., strings. 5 minutes.

Uunpublished; score and parts available from Heroico Music Publications.

Originally sketched for piano (*see:* W88)

PREMIERE

W10a. 1941 (January 23); Rochester, New York; Rochester Symphony Orchestra; Dr. Howard Hanson, conductor.

W11. *Drouth* (1939) Chicago

3-2-2-2, 4-3-3-1, timp., perc., strings. 6 minutes.

Unpublished; score and parts available from the Fleisher Collection. Additional copy of the score available from the American Heritage Center (University of Wyoming).

Selected for Composer's Forum, Dallas Public Library, 9 February 1958

W11a. 1942 (February 23); Chicago; Illinois Symphony Orchestra; Dr. Kurt Herbert Adler, conductor. *See:* B100.

W11b. 1958 (February 9); Dallas, Texas; Dallas Symphony Orchestra; Walter Hendl, conductor.

W11c. 1960 (February 21); Madrid; Madrid Symphony Orchestra; Vincente Spiteri, conductor.

W11d. 1979; Downey, California; Downey Symphony Orchestra; Dr. Luis Palange, conductor.

W12. *Ontonagon Sketches* **(Sunset on Lake Michigan; Woods At Dusk; Victoria Falls)** (1939) Ontonagon, Michigan

3-3-3-3, 4-3-3-1, timp., perc., strings. 20 minutes.

Published by Seesaw Music Corporation. Score and parts also available from the Fleisher Collection. Additional copy of the score for "Woods At Dusk" available from the Library of Congress.

First prize, San Antonio (Texas) Musical Club, December 10, 1942.

W13. *Pastorale* (1939) Chicago

2-3-2-2, 2-2-0-0, timp. perc., strings. 7 minutes.

Unpublished; score and parts available from the Fleisher Collection. Additional copy of the score available from the American Heritage Center (University of Wyoming).

W13a. 1954 (May 23); Whittier, California; Whittier Symphony Orchestra; Ruth Haroldson, conductor.

W13b. 1966 (June 12); Los Angeles; Brentwood-Westwood Symphony Orchestra; Alvin Mills, conductor.

W13c. 1966 (October 30); La Jolla, California; La Jolla Civic Orchestra; Alvin Mills, conductor.

W14. *Saturnale* (1939) Chicago

3-3-3-3, 4-3-3-1, timp., perc., strings. 18 minutes.

Unpublished; score and parts available from the Fleisher Collection. Additional copy of the score available from the UCLA Music Library.

PREMIERE

W14a. date unknown, rehearsal with Chicago Symphony Orchestra, Frederick Stock, conductor.

W14b. 1957 (February 19); Washington, D.C.; United States Air Force Symphony; Colonel George Howard, conductor. *See:* B123, 124, 125.

W15. *Prison (Lament)* for Violin and Small Orchestra (1940) Chicago

2-1-2-1, 1-2-0-0, timp., strings. 3 minutes.

Published by Seesaw Music Corporation. Score and parts also available from the Fleisher Collection. Additional copy of the score available from the Library of Congress. Original blueprint score included in the Moldenhauer Collection, Harvard University.

Originally for violin and piano (*see:* W47).

PREMIERE

W15a. 1940 (November 15); Chicago; Lane High School Orchestra, Joseph Grill, conductor.

OTHER SELECTED PERFORMANCES

W15b. 1941 (June); Hollywood, California; Studio orchestra broadcast on KFI radio; Claude Sweeten, conductor.

W15c. 1941 (June 18); Los Angeles; Los Angeles Woman's Symphony Orchestra; Ruth Haroldson, conductor.

W15d. 1941 (July 29); San Diego, California; San Diego Symphony Orchestra; Dr. Nikolai Sokoloff, conductor. *See:* B95.

W15e. 1946 (February 5); Amarillo, Texas; Amarillo Symphony Orchestra; Robert Barron, conductor. *See:* B102.

W15f. 1961 (May 6); Los Angeles; Wilshire Symphony Orchestra; Arthur Lipkin, conductor.

W15g. 1962 (May 6); Los Angeles; Wilshire Symphony Orchestra; Victor DePinto, conductor.

W15h. 1964 (December 13); Sacramento, California; Sacramento Symphony Orchestra; James A. Adair, conductor.

W15i. 1967 (April 30); Palm Desert, California; Palm Desert Symphony Orchestra; Thomas Mancini, conductor.

W15j. 1967 (May 28); Los Angeles; Brentwood Symphony Orchestra; Alvin Mills, conductor.

W15k. 1967 (August 18); Redlands, California; Idyllwild Symphony Orchestra; Alvin MIlls, conductor.

W15l. 1967 (August 20); Idyllwild, California; Idyllwild Youth Symphony Orchestra; Alvin Mills, conductor.

W15m. 1974 (January 12); Tokyo; Youth Symphony Orchestra of Japan; Arthur Lipkin, conductor.

W15n. 1981; Beverly Hills, California; Los Angeles Council of Music and Art Symphony Orchestra; Dr. Bolet, conductor.

W16. Suite For Strings (Nostalgia, Serenade, Consecration) (1940)
Coronado, California

16 minutes.

Unpublished; score and parts available from the Fleisher Collection. Additional copy of the score for "Nostalgia" available from the American Heritage Center (University of Wyoming).

First National Prize, Sigma Alpha Iota, June 9, 1941. *See:* B96.

PREMIERE

W16a. 1945 (October 23); Rochester, New York; Rochester Philharmonic Orchestra; Dr. Howard Hanson, conductor.

OTHER SELECTED PERFORMANCES

W16b. 1983 (March 6); Los Angeles; Brentwood-Westwood Symphony Orchestra; Alvin Mills, conductor.

W17. *Saint Francis of Assisi* (1941) Coronado, California

2-2-2-2, 4-3-3-1, timp., perc., strings. 7 minutes.

Unpublished; score and parts available from the Fleisher Collection. Additional copies of the score available from the American Heritage Center (University of Wyoming); UCLA Music Library.

PREMIERE

W17a.   1961 (October 27); Hawthorne, California; Hollywood Symphony Orchestra; Dr. Ernest Gebert, conductor. *See:* B132.

OTHER SELECTED PERFORMANCES

W17b.   1961 (October 28); Hollywood, California; Hollywood Symphony Orchestra; Dr. Ernest Gebert, conductor.

W17c.   1962 (January 18); Washington, D.C.; United States Air Force Symphony Orchestra; Colonel George Howard, conductor.

W18.   *San Luis Rey* (1941)   Coronado, California

3-2-2-2, 4-3-3-1, timp., perc., strings.   4 minutes.

Unpublished; score and parts available from the Fleisher Collection. Additional copy of the score available from the UCLA Music Library.

PREMIERE

W18a.   1944 (January 9); Whittier, California; Whittier Symphony Orchestra; Ruth Haroldson, conductor. *See:* B101.

OTHER SELECTED PERFORMANCES

W18b.   1944 (April 9, 12); Los Angeles; Los Angeles Woman's Symphony; Ruth Haroldson, conductor.

W18c.   1947 (April 7); Glendale, California; Glendale Symphony Orchestra; Scipione Guidi, conductor. *See:* B103.

W19.   *Phantasy for Oboe and Orchestra* (1942)   Coronado, California

2-2-2-2, 2-2-2-1, timp., perc., strings.   8 minutes.

Unpublished; score and parts available from Heroico Music Publications.

Originally for oboe and piano (*see:* W50).

Second prize, National Composers Clinic 1950.

W19a. 1958 (April 22); Amarillo, Texas; Amarillo Symphony Orchestra; A. Clyde Roller, soloist, George Bledsoe, conductor.

W20. *We Believe* (1942) Hollywood

3-3-2-3, 4-3-3-1, timp. perc., strings. 6 minutes.

Unpublished; score and parts available from Heroico Music Publications.

First National Prize, Delta Omicron International Fraternity, June 8, 1945.

Inspired by the San Bernardino Mountains of California.

PREMIERE

W20a. 1961 (March 19); Madrid, Spain; Madrid Symphony Orchestra; Vicente Spiteri, conductor.

W21. *Jewels of Lake Tahoe* (1945) Hollywood

2-1-1-2, 2-2-2-1, timp., perc., strings. 5 minutes.

Unpublished; score and parts available from the Fleisher Collection. Additional copies of the score available from the American Heritage Center (University of Wyoming); UCLA Music Library.

W22. *Red Clay* (1946) Hollywood

3-2-2-3, 4-3-3-1, timp., perc., strings. 7 minutes.

Unpublished; score and parts available from Heroico Music Publications. *See:* B108.

W23. *Serenata Sorrentina* for Small Orchestra (1946) Hollywood

2-1-1-2, 2-2-2-0, timp., perc., strings. 3 minutes.

Unpublished; score and parts available from Heroico Music Publications. Additional copy of the score available from the UCLA Music Library.

w23a. 1947 (April 8); Amarillo, Texas; Amarillo Symphony Orchestra; Robert Barron, conductor. *See:* B104.

OTHER SELECTED PERFORMANCES

w23b. 1954 (November 21); Jacksonville, Alabama; Northern Alabama Symphony Orchestra; Robert Brown, conductor.

w23c. 1954 (November 29); Gadsdan, Alabama; Northern Alabama Symphony Orchestra; Robert Brown, conductor.

w23d. 1954 (December 6); Anniston, Alabama; Northern Alabama Symphony Orchestra; Robert Brown, conductor.

W24. *Umpqua Forest* (1946) Hollywood

3-2-2-3, 4-3-2-1, timp. perc., strings. 8 minutes.

Unpublished; score and parts available from Heroico Music Publications.

W25. *Paint Horse and Saddle* (1947) Hollywood

2-2-2-2, 4-3-3-1, timp., perc., strings. 7 minutes.

Unpublished; score and parts available from Heroico Music Publications. Additional copy of the score available from the Library of Congress.

Originally sketched for piano (*see:* W97)

W26. *Chicken In The Rough* (1951) Hollywood

2-1-2-1, 2-2-2-1, timp., perc., strings. 4 minutes.

Unpublished; score and parts available from Heroico Music Publications.

Originally sketched for piano (*see:* W107)

W27. *Cactus Rhapsody* (1953) Hollywood

2-2-2-2, 4-2-2-1, timp., perc., strings. 8 minutes.

Unpublished; score and parts available from the Fleisher Collection.

Originally for solo piano (*see:* W109).

PREMIERE

W27a. 1960 (April 4); Washington, D.C.; United States Air Force Symphony Orchestra; Captain John F. Yesulaitis, conductor.

OTHER SELECTED PERFORMANCES

W27b. 1975 (October 19); Los Angeles; Brentwood-Westwood Symphony Orchestra; Alvin Mills, conductor.

The Earth Does Not Wish For Beauty [chorus and orchestra] 1953. *See:* W181.

W28. *Angel Chimes* (1954) Hollywood

1-1-1-1, 1-1-0-0, cymbals, celesta or piano, strings. 3 minutes.

Unpublished; score and parts available from Heroico Music Publications.

Originally for solo piano (*see:* W106).

PREMIERE

W28a. 1961 (March 1); Washington, D.C.; United States Air Force Symphony Orchestra; Major Arnold D. Gabriel, conductor.

W29. *Solar Joy* (formerly *Radiation)* (1955) Hollywood

3-2-2-2, 4-3-3-1, timp., perc., strings. 4 minutes.

Unpublished; score and parts available from Heroico Music Publications.

Originally for solo piano (*see:* W112).

W30. *Cowboy Rhapsody* (1956) Hollywood

3-2-2-2, 4-3-3-1, timp., perc., strings. 13 minutes.

Unpublished; score and parts available from the Fleisher Collection. Additional copies of the score available from the Library of Congress; UCLA Music Library.

Dedicated to the pioneers of West Texas.

PREMIERE

W30a. 1956 (April 11); Amarillo, Texas; Amarillo Symphony Orchestra; A. Clyde Roller, conductor. *See:* B119, 120, 121, 122, 125, 126.

OTHER SELECTED PERFORMANCES

W30b. 1959 (March 18); Washington, D.C.; United States Air Force Symphony Orchestra; Colonel George Howard, conductor.

W30c. 1980 (March 2); Los Angeles; Brentwood-Westwood Symphony Orchestra; Alvin Mills, conductor.

W31. *Minha Terra* (Barrozo Netto) (1958) Hollywood

2-2-2-2, 3-2-2-1, timp., perc., strings. 4 minutes.

Unpublished; score and parts available from Heroico Music Publications.

Originally for two pianos (*see:* W143)

Arranged from a work by Brazilian composer Barrozo Netto.

PREMIERE

W31a. 1965 (May 31); Washington, D.C.; United States Air Force Symphony Orchestra; Major Arnold D. Gabriel, conductor.

W32. *This Is The Place* (1958) Hollywood

2-2-2-2, 4-3-3-1, timp., perc., strings. 5 minutes.

Unpublished; score and parts available from Heroico Music Publications. Additional copy of the score available from the Library of Congress.

Inspired by Brigham Young's exclamation upon reaching Utah after crossing the continent in covered wagons.

Nissan [chorus and orchestra] 1961. *See:* W187.

W33. *Cosmic Mist Symphony* (In The Beginning, Nebula, Nuclear Fission) (1962) Hollywood

3-2-2-2, 4-3-3-1, timp., perc., strings.   24 minutes.

Unpublished; score and parts available from the Fleisher Collection. Original pencil score of "Nebula" included in the Moldenhauer Collection, Harvard University.

First National Prize, National League of American Pen Women, 1964.
Selected for the "Symposium of New Music" sponsored by the University of Houston in cooperation with the Houston Symphony Society under a grant from the Rockefeller Foundation in Houston, Texas April 18-25, 1967. *See:* B136, 137.

PREMIERE

W33a. 1967 (April 18); Houston, Texas; Houston Symphony Orchestra; A. Clyde Roller, conductor. *See:* B136, 137.

OTHER SELECTED PERFORMANCES

W33b. 1968 (November 10); Miller Theater, Hermann Park, Houston, Texas; University of Houston Symphony Orchestra; A. Clyde Roller, conductor.

W34. *Kambu* (1963) Hollywood

2-2-2-2, 4-3-3-1, timp., perc., strings. 8 minutes.

Unpublished; score and parts available from Heroico Music Publications.

Originally a ballet for piano and narrator (*see:* W159).

W35. *Little per cent* (1963) Aspen, Colorado; Hollywood

2-2-2-2, 4-3-3-1, timp., perc., strings. 4 minutes.

Unpublished; score and parts available from Heroico Music Publications. Additional copy of the score available from the American Heritage Center (University of Wyoming). Original pencil sketch included in the Moldenhauer Collection, Harvard University.

Brothers of the Clouds [chorus and orchestra] 1964. *See:* W191.

W36. *Les Fameux Douze* **(The Famous Twelve)** for Small Orchestra (1965) Hollywood

1-1-1-1, 0-0-1-1, strings. 5 minutes.

Unpublished; score and parts available from Heroico Music Publications. Additional copy of the score available from the UCLA Music Library.

First National Prize, National League of American Pen Women, 1966.

Written after hearing a debate on the twelve-tone method.

W37. *Pyramids of Giza* (1973) Hollywood

1-1-1-1, 1-1, perc., strings. 8 minutes.

Unpublished; score and parts available from Heroico Music Publications.

Originally for solo piano (*see: Egyptian Suite* W123).

First National Prize, National League of American Pen Women, Washington, D.C., April 10, 1976.

PREMIERE

W37a. 1976 (February 20); New York; Greenwich Symphony Orchestra; Michael Bartos, conductor.

W38. *Alaskan Trail of '98* (1980) Hollywood

For concert band. 8 minutes.

Unpublished; score and parts available from Heroico Music Publications.

Originally for solo piano (*see:* W122).

The Builders [chorus and orchestra] 1978. *See:* W207.

W39. *Anwar Sadat (In Memory)* (1982) Hollywood

2-2-2-2, 3-3-3-1, perc., strings. 8 minutes.

Unpublished; score and parts available from the Fleisher Collection.

Originally for solo piano (*see:* W130).

Mother [narrator and orchestra] 1982. *See:* W279.

W40. *Earth of God* for String Orchestra (1984) Hollywood

9 minutes.

Unpublished; score and parts available from the Fleisher Collection.

Originally for solo piano (*see:* W134).

W41. *Sam Houston* (1987) Hollywood

2-2-2-2, 4-3-3-1, timp., perc., strings. 18 minutes.

Unpublished; score and parts available from Heroico Music Publications.

Originally for solo piano (*see:* W137).

W42. *Texas* (1987) Hollywood

2-2-2-2, 4-3-3-1, timp., perc., strings. 18 minutes.

Unpublished; score and parts available from the Fleisher Collection.

CHAMBER ENSEMBLE

W43. *Portrait of Thomas Jefferson* (formerly titled *Epic Poem)* (1927) Chicago

String quartet. 8 minutes.

Unpublished; score and parts available from Heroico Music Publications. Additional copies of the score available from the UCLA Music Library; San Francisco Conservatory.

First National Award, National League of American Pen Women, 1936. *See:* B67.
First National Prize, Music Teachers Association of California, April 21, 1960.

PREMIERE

W43a. 1927; Chicago; Girvin String Quartet.

OTHER SELECTED PERFORMANCES

W43b. 1936 (April 17); Performed at the White House. *See:* B67.

W43c. 1936 (May 4); Chicago; The American String Quartet (WPA-sponsored).

W43d. 1962 (January 26); Hollywood, California; Parnassus Quartet.

W43e. 1962 (September 18); Hollywood, California; Woman's Chamber Music Society.

W43f. 1979 (September 9); Los Angeles; Brentwood-Westwood String Quartet (for Radie Britain Day).

W43g. 1982 (March 27); Rome.

W44. *Legend* (1928) Chicago

Violin and piano. 3 minutes.

Unpublished; score and parts available from Heroico Music Publications.

First National Prize, National League of American Pen Women, 1952.

W45. *Dance Grotesque* (1929) Chicago

Violin and piano. 4 minutes.

Unpublished; score and parts available from Heroico Music Publications.

Originally for solo piano (*see:* W84).

W46. String Quartet (Allegro ma Grazioso, Adagio, Scherzando, Allegro) (1934) Chicago

18 minutes.

Unpublished; score and parts available from Heroico Music Publications. Additional copies of the score available from the American Heritage Center (University of Wyoming); UCLA Music Library.

First National Prize, National League of American Pen Women, 1938. *See:* B93.
First State Prize of Illinois, Lake View Musical Society, 1940.

PREMIERE

w46a.   1940 (November 3); Chicago; Lake View String Quartet. *See:* B93.

OTHER SELECTED PERFORMANCES

w46b.   1942 (March 15); Los Angeles; Robert Pollock Quartet. *See:* W98.

w46c.   1956 (November 18); Fort Meyer, Arlington, Virginia; United States Army Band Quartet.

w46d.   1962 (January 16); Santa Monica, California; Parnassus Quartet.   (Dawn Adams Phelps, violin; Alice Willardson, violin; Emma Hardy Hill, viola; Helen Humphrey, cello).

w46e.   1962 (January 21); Hollywood, California; Parnassus Quartet.

w46f.   1962 (March 23); Los Angeles; Parnassus Quartet

w46g.   1962 (May 5); Los Angeles; Parnassus Quartet.

W47. *Prison (Lament)*   (1935) Chicago

Violin and piano. 3 minutes.

Published by Neil Kjos (Chicago). Additional copies of the score available from the Amarillo Public Library; New York Public Library; Northwestern University Library, Evanston, Ill.; Library of Congress; Texas Composers Collection (University of Texas). Copy of the manuscript available from the Library of Congress.

PREMIERE

w47a. 1935 (November 5); Chicago; Richard Czerwonky, violin.

W48. *The Chateau* (1938) Chicago

Violin and piano. 4 minutes.

Unpublished; score and parts available from Heroico Music Publications.

Originally for solo piano (*see:* W86).

W49. *Chipmunks* (1940) Hollywood

Woodwind, harp and percussion. 3 minutes.

Unpublished; score and parts available from Heroico Music Publications.

First National Prize, National League of American Pen Women, 1964

W50. *Dance Grotesque* (1940) Hollywood

Two flutes. 4 minutes.

Published by Seesaw Music Corporation. Additional copy of the score available from the Library of Congress.

Originally for solo piano (*see:* W84).

W51. *Phantasy* (1942) Hollywood

Oboe and piano. 8 minutes.

Published by Seesaw Music Corporation. Additional copies of the score available from the American Music Center; UCLA Music Library.

Texas Composer's Guild Award, 1978

W52. *Phantasy* (1942) Hollywood

Oboe, harp and piano. 8 minutes.

Unpublished; score and parts available from Heroico Music Publications.

Originally for oboe and piano (*see:* W51).

First National Prize, National League of American Pen Women, 1978

W53. *Serenade* (1944) Chicago

Violin and piano. 3 minutes.

Unpublished; score and parts available from Heroico Music Publications. Additional copy of the score available from the UCLA Music Library.

Originally for solo voice (*see:* W236).

First prize, Music Teachers Association of California, 1955

W54. *Barcarola* (1948) Chicago

Violin and piano. 5 minutes.

Unpublished; score and parts available from Heroico Music Publications. Additional copies of the score available from the Amarillo Public Library; UCLA Music Library.

Based on a theme from *Saturnale,* W14. *See:* B116.

First National Prize, National League of American Pen Women, 1960

W55. *Intermezzo* (1950) Hollywood

Oboe, clarinet, horn, bassoon and piano. 7 minutes.

Unpublished; score and parts available from Heroico Music Publications.

Originally for orchestra (*see: Symphonic Intermezzo,* W2).

W56. *Casa del Sogno* (1955) Hollywood

Violin and piano. 4 minutes.

Unpublished; score and parts available from Heroico Music Publications. Additional copy of the score available from the American Heritage Center (University of Wyoming).

W57. *Barcarola* (1958) Hollywood

Eight celli and vocalise. 5 minutes.

Published by Seesaw Music Corporation. Additional copy of the score available from the UCLA Music Library.

Originally for violin and piano (*see:* W54).

First National Prize, Arizona Cello Society, June 1, 1974.

W57a. 1975 (May 17); Tempe, Arizona; Arizona Cello Society Orchestra; Jerome Kessler, guest conductor; Cathy Dockendorff, soprano.

OTHER SELECTED PERFORMANCES

W57b. 1981 (July 31); Laguna Beach, California; Laguna Beach Summer Music Festival, Masatoski Mitsumata, Music Director; Christine Walevska, solo cello.

W58. *Casa Del Sogno* (1958) Hollywood

Oboe and piano. 4 minutes.

Unpublished; score and parts available from Heroico Music Publications. Additional copy of the score available from the UCLA Music Library.

Originally for violin and piano (*see:* W56).

W59. *In The Beginning* (1962) Hollywood

Four horns. 6 minutes.

Published by Seesaw Music Corporation. Additional copies of the score available from the Amarillo Public Library; American Heritage Center (University of Wyoming). Original pencil sketch included in the Moldenhauer Collection, Harvard University.

First National Prize, National League of American Pen Women, 1964.

PREMIERE

W59a. 1980 (May 27); New York; Women's National Convention.

W60. *Four Sarabandes* (1965) Hollywood

Woodwind quintet. 8 minutes.

Published by Seesaw Music Corporation. Original score located at the Library of Congress.

Originally for solo piano (*see:* W118).

For students.

W61. *Les Fameux Douze (The Famous 12)* (1966) Hollywood

Violin and cello. 5 minutes.

Unpublished; score and parts available from Heroico Music Publications. Additional copy of the score available from the UCLA Music Library.

Originally for small orchestra (*see:* W36).

W62. *Pastorale* (1967) Hollywood

Recorder, oboe, harp, and harpsichord. 9 minutes.

Unpublished; score and parts available from Heroico Music Publications. Additional copy of the score available from the UCLA Music Library. Original score located at the Library of Congress.

Originally for orchestra (*see:* W13).

W63. *Awake To Life* (1968) Hollywood

Brass quintet. 4 minutes.

Published by Trombone Association Publications. Additional copy of the score available from the UCLA Music Library.

Originally for chorus (*see:* W188).

Second prize, Texas Federation of Music Clubs, Corpus Christi, Texas, 1968.

W64. *Processional* (1969) Hollywood

Four trombones. 3 minutes.

Published by Harold Branch Publishing Co.

W65. *Recessional*   (1969) Hollywood

Four trombones. 3 minutes.

Published by Harold Branch Publishing Co.

Overtones [voice and flute] 1970. *See:* W264.

W66. *Phantasy*   (1970) Hollywood

Flute and piano. 8 minutes.

Unpublished; score and parts available from Heroico Music Publications.

Originally for oboe and piano (*see:* W51).

First National Prize, National League of American Pen Women, 1972.

W67. *Phantasy*   (1974) Hollywood

Clarinet, oboe and bassoon. 8 minutes.

Unpublished; score and parts available from Heroico Music Publications. Additional copies of the score available from the UCLA Music Library;   California State University, Dominguez Hills, Music Library.

Originally for oboe and piano (*see:* W51).

W68. *The Earth Does Not Wish for Beauty*   (1975) Hollywood. Text by Lester Luther.

Voice, 2 trumpets, horn, trombone and tuba. 6 minutes.

Unpublished; score and parts available from Heroico Music Publications.

Originally for solo voice and piano (*see:* W230).

W69. *Pastorale*   (1975) Hollywood

Flute and harp. 9 minutes.

Unpublished; score and parts available from Heroico Music Publications. Additional copy of the score available from the UCLA Music Library.

Originally for orchestra (*see:* W13).

PREMIERE

W69a. 1979 (August 1); Stockholm, Sweden; Georgia Mohammar, harp; Gloria Lundell, flute.

W70. *Rhumbando* (1975) Hollywood

Wind ensemble. 4 minutes.

Unpublished; score and parts available from Heroico Music Publications. Additional copy of the score available from the UCLA Music Library. Original score included in the Moldenhauer Collection, Harvard University.

Originally for orchestra as third movement of the *Southern Symphony*, (*see:* W9).

PREMIERE

W70a. 1970 (November 6); Washington, D.C.; United States Air Force Ensemble, Major Arnold D. Gabriel, conductor.

W71. *Adoration* (1976) Hollywood

Two trumpets, horn and trombone. 6 minutes.

Published by Trombone Association Publications. Additional copy of the score available from the UCLA Library.

Originally for solo piano (*see:* W114).

W72. *Hebraic Poem* (1976) Hollywood

String quartet. 15 minutes.

Unpublished; score and parts available from Heroico Music Publications.

Honorable Mention, National League of American Pen Women, Boston, April 1986.

W73. *Cactus Rhapsody* (1977) Hollywood

Clarinet, cello, piano. 8 minutes.

Unpublished; score and parts available from Heroico Music Publications. Additional copy of the score available from the UCLA Library. Original pencil sketch included in the Moldenhauer Collection, Harvard University.

Originally for solo piano (*see:* W109).

First National Prize, National League of American Pen Women, Sacramento, California, 1978.

PREMIERE

W73a. 1978 (April 17); Washington, D.C.; National Convention, National League of American Pen Women.

W74. *The Earth Does Not Wish for Beauty* (1977) Hollywood

Four tubas. 6 minutes.

Published by Trombone Association Publications. Original pencil score included in the Moldenhauer Collection, Harvard University.

Originally for solo voice (*see:* W230).

W75. *Dance Grotesque* (1979) Hollywood

Flute and piano. 4 minutes.

Unpublished but available from Heroico Music Publications.

Originally for solo piano (*see:* W84).

PREMIERE

W75a. 1979 (September 9); Los Angeles, California.

W76. *Prison (Lament)* (1979) Hollywood

String quartet. 4 minutes.

Published by Heroico Music Publications. Additional copy of the score available from the UCLA Music Library.

Originally for violin and piano (*see:* W47).

W77. *Translunar Cycle* **(Space Walk, Moonscape, Earthrise)** (1980) Hollywood

Cello and piano. 10 minutes.

Unpublished but available from Heroico Music Publications. Additional copy of the score available from the UCLA Library.

Originally for solo voice (*see:* W265).

Selected for Festival of Texas Composers, North Texas State University, February 25-26, 1982.

PREMIERE

W77a. 1982 (February 25); Denton, Texas; Diego Villa, cello; Chung Lu, piano.

W78. *Ode To NASA* (1981) Hollywood

Brass quintet. 8 minutes.

Published by Trombone Association Publications.

W79. *Soul Of The Sea* (1984) Hollywood

Cello and piano. 8 minutes.

Unpublished but available from Heroico Music Publications.

W80. Suite for String Quartet (Nostalgia, Serenade, Consecration) (1989) Hollywood

Score and parts unpublished but available from Heroico Music Publications.

Originally for string orchestra (*see:* W16).

SOLO PIANO

W81. *Ocean Moods* (1925) Amarillo

Unpublished.

First serious composition.

PREMIERE

W81a. 1928 (February 10); Amarillo, Texas; Radie Britain.

W82. *Prelude* (1925) Munich

Published by Otto Halbreiter (Germany) and Heroico Music Publications (United States) Additional copy available from the Texas Composers Collection (University of Texas).

PREMIERE

w82a. 1926 (December 9); Chicago; Radie Britain. *See:* B24, 26, 27.

OTHER SELECTED PERFORMANCES

w82b. 1928 (February 10); Amarillo, Texas; Radie Britain. *See:* B49.

W83. *Western Suite* **(On the Plains, Covered Wagon, Mirage, Campfire, Stampede)** (1925) Munich

Published by Otto Halbreiter (Germany) and Heroico Music Publications (United States); "Covered Wagon" published separately by Neil Kjos (Chicago). Additional copy of "Covered Wagon" available from the Texas Composers Collection (University of Texas).

PREMIERE

w83a. 1926 (December 9); Chicago; Radie Britain. *See:* B24, 25, 26, 27, 29.

OTHER SELECTED PERFORMANCES

w83b. 1928 (February 10); Amarillo, Texas; Radie Britain. *See:* B49.

W84. *Dance Grotesque* (1929) Chicago

Unpublished but available from Heroico Music Publications. Additional copy available from the UCLA Music Library.

W85. *Infant Suite* **(The Infant, Berceuse, Toy Parade)** (1935) Chicago

Unpublished but available from Heroico Music Publications.

W86. *The Chateau* (1938) Palo Duro Canyon, Texas

Unpublished but available from Heroico Music Publications.

W87. *Little Spaniard* (1938) Chicago

Published by Summy Birchard (first published by Arthur P. Schmidt).

For second grade.

W88. *Canyon* (1939) Chicago

Piano sketch used for orchestration; not intended as piano solo (*see:* W10). Copy available from the New York Public Library.

W89. *Drouth* (1939) Chicago

Unpublished but available from Heroico Music Publications.

Originally for orchestra (*see:* W11).

W90. *Geppetto's Toy Shop* (1940) Chicago

Published by Summy Birchard (first published by Arthur P. Schmidt).

For second grade.

W91. *Serenada Del Coronado* (1940) Coronado, California.

Unpublished but available from Heroico Music Publications. Additional copies available from the Amarillo Public Library; UCLA Music Library.

W92. *Saint Francis Of Assisi* (1941) Coronado, California

Unpublished but available from Heroico Music Publications.

Originally for orchestra (*see:* W17).

W93. *San Luis Rey* (1941) Coronado California

Unpublished but available from Heroico Music Publications. Additional copies available from the New York Public Library; UCLA Music Library.

Originally for orchestra (*see:* W18).

W94. *Dance of the Clown* (1945) Hollywood

Published by Summy Birchard (first published by Arthur P. Schmidt).

For second grade.

W95. *Red Clay* (1946) Hollywood

Unpublished but available from Heroico Music Publications. Additional copy available from the New York Public Library.

Originally for orchestra (*see:* W22).

W96. *Serenata Sorrentina* (1946) Hollywood

Unpublished but available from Heroico Music Publications. Additional copy available from the New York Public Library.

Originally for orchestra (*see:* W23).

W97. *Paint Horse and Saddle* (1947) Hollywood

Piano sketch used for orchestration; not intended as piano solo (*see:* W25). Copy available from the New York Public Library.

W98. *Barcarola* (1948) Hollywood

Unpublished but available from Heroico Music Publications.

Originally for violin and piano (*see:* W54).

W99. *Goddess of Inspiration* (1948) Hollywood

Unpublished but available from Heroico Music Publications. Additional copy available from the UCLA Music Library.

Originally for solo voice (*see:* W242).

W100. *The Juggler* (1948) Hollywood

Unpublished but available from Heroico Music Publications.

W101. *Enchantment* (1949) Hollywood

Unpublished but available from Heroico Music Publications. Additional copy available from the UCLA Music Library.

W102. *Escape* (1949) Hollywood

Unpublished but available from Heroico Music Publications. Additional copies available from the American Heritage Center (University of Wyoming); Library of Congress; UCLA Music Library.

Dedicated to Rupert Hughes.

W103. *Heel and Toe* (1949) Hollywood

Unpublished but available from Heroico Music Publications.

W104. *Torillo* (1949) Hollywood

Published by Heroico Music Publications.

W105. *How To Play the Piano* (1950) Hollywood

Published by Walter T. Foster. Additional copies available from the Amarillo Public Library; New York Public Library.

W106. *Angel Chimes* (1951) Hollywood

Published by American Music Edition. Additional copy available from the American Heritage Center (University of Wyoming).

W107. *Chicken in the Rough* (1951) Hollywood

Piano sketch used for orchestration; not intended as piano solo (*see:* W26). Copy available from the New York Public Library.

W108. *Wings of Silver* (1951) Hollywood

Published by Willis Music Company. Additional copy available from the Amarillo Public Library.

W109. *Cactus Rhapsody* (1953) Hollywood

Unpublished but available from Heroico Music Publications. Additional copies available from the New York Public Library; UCLA Music Library.

W110. *Joy* (1953) Hollywood

Unpublished but available from Heroico Music Publications.

W111. Reflections (1953) Hollywood

Unpublished but available from Heroico Music Publications. Additional copy available from the UCLA Music Library.

W112. *Solar Joy* (formerly titled ***Radiation***) (1953) Hollywood

Unpublished but available from Heroico Music Publications. Additional copies available from the Amarillo Public Library; American Heritage Center (University of Wyoming); UCLA Music Library.

W113. *Mexican Weaver* (1954) Hollywood

Unpublished but available from Heroico Music Publications. Additional copy available from the Library of Congress.

W114. *Adoration* (1955) Hollywood

Published by Heroico Music Publications. Additional copy available from the UCLA Music Library.

W115. *Ensenada* (1956) Hollywood

Published by Ricordi and Sons, Brazil. Additional copy available from the UCLA Music Library.

W116. *Song Of The Joshua* (1956) Hollywood

Unpublished but available from Heroico Music Publications.

W117. Sonata, Op. 17 (1958) Hollywood

Unpublished but available from Heroico Music Publications. Additional copies available from the American Heritage Center (University of Wyoming); UCLA Music Library.

First prize, Texas Federation of Music Clubs 1958.
First prize, National League of American Pen Women, 1959.
First prize, Music Teachers Association of California, 1959.

W118. *Four Sarabandes* (1963) Hollywood

Unpublished but available from Heroico Music Publications. Additional copy available from the Texas Federation of Music Clubs Music Manuscript Archive, Dallas Public Library.

W119. *Les Fameux Douze (The Famous 12)* (1965) Hollywood

Unpublished but available from Heroico Music Publications.

W120. *Epiphyllum* (1966) Hollywood

Published by Heroico Music Publications.

W121. *Ridin' Herd In Texas* (1966) Hollywood

Published by Heroico Music Publications (originally published by Robert B. Brown, Hollywood). Additional copy available from the Carson County Square House Museum.

Dedicated to Blanche and Edgar Britain, Jr., of the Lazy⊓ Ranch, five miles from Stinnett, Texas.

W122. *Alaskan Trail of '98* (1967) Hollywood

Unpublished but available from Heroico Music Publications. Additional copies available from the American Heritage Center (University of Wyoming); UCLA Music Library.

W123. *Egyptian Suite (Obeliske, The River Nile, Pyramids of Giza)* (1969) Hollywood

Unpublished but available from Heroico Music Publications. Additional copies available from the American Heritage Center (University of Wyoming); UCLA Music Library.

W124. *Lakalani* (1970) Hollywood

Published in Pen Women magazine. Available from Heroico Music Publications.

Dedicated to Lerae Britain.

W125. *Hawaiian Chants: Pianorama of Hawai'i* (1971) Hollywood

Unpublished but available from Heroico Music Publications.

33 short compositions. Includes a history of Hawaiian chants written by Lerae Britain.

W126. *Invocation* (1977) Hollywood

Unpublished but available from Heroico Music Publications.

W127. *Kuilima* (1977) Hollywood

Unpublished but available from Heroico Music Publications. Additional copy available from the UCLA Music Library.

W128. *Lei of Love* (1978) Hollywood

Unpublished but available from Heroico Music Publications. Additional copy available from the UCLA Music Library.

Dedicated to Lerae Britain.

W129. *AdáKris* (1981) Hollywood

Unpublished but available from Heroico Music Publications.

Dedicated to Edward Bush.

W130. *Anwar Sadat* (1981) Hollywood

Unpublished but available from Heroico Music Publications.

W131. *After The Storm* (1982) Hollywood

Unpublished but available from Heroico Music Publications.

W132. *Alaskan Inner Passage* (1983) Hollywood

Unpublished but available from Heroico Music Publications.

W133. *Surf and Sand* (1983) Hollywood

Unpublished but available from Heroico Music Publications.

PREMIERE

W133a. 1985 (March 28); Kansas Congress of Composers.

W134. *Earth of God* (1984) Hollywood

Unpublished but available from Heroico Music Publications.

W135. *Neutrinos* (1985) Hollywood

Unpublished but available from Heroico Music Publications.

W136. *Upbeat* (1985) Hollywood

Unpublished but available from Heroico Music Publications.

W137. *Sam Houston* (1986) Hollywood

Unpublished but available from Heroico Music Publications.

W138. *Epiphyllum* (for left hand) (1987) Hollywood

Unpublished but available from Heroico Music Publications.

Originally for solo piano, two hands (*see:* W120).

W139. *Upbeat* (for third grade) (1988) Hollywood

Unpublished but available from Heroico Music Publications.

Originally for (ungraded) solo piano (*see:* W136).

TWO PIANOS

W140. *Pastorale* (1939)   Chicago

Unpublished but available from Heroico Music Publications. Additional copies available from the American Heritage Center (University of Wyoming); UCLA Music Library. Signed blueprint copies included in the Moldenhauer Collection, Harvard University.

Originally for orchestra (*see:* W13).

First Prize, Illinois Federation of Music Clubs, March 17, 1940.

W141. *Rhapsodic Phantasie* (1950) Hollywood

8 minutes.

Unpublished but available from Heroico Music Publications. Additional copy available from the UCLA Music Library.

Originally for piano and orchestra (*see:* W4).

W142. *Angel Chimes* (1951) Hollywood

Unpublished but available from Heroico Music Publications.

Originally for solo piano (*see:* W106).

W143. *Minha Terra* (Barrozo Netto) (1956) Hollywood

Published by Ricordi and Sons, Brazil.

Arranged from a work by Brazilian composers Barrozo Netto. See: B125, 127.

W144. *Le Petit Concerto* (1957) Hollywood

Published by Heroico Music Publications. Additional copy available from the Texas Federation of Music Clubs Music Manuscript Archive, Dallas Public Library.

W145. *Cactus Rhapsody* (1965) Hollywood

Unpublished but available from Heroico Music Publications. Pencil manuscript located at the Library of Congress.

Originally for solo piano (*see:* W109).

HARP

Love Song of the Taj Mahal [narrator and harp] 1947. *See:* W239.

W146. *Reflection* (1965) Hollywood

Published by Heroico Music Publications. Additional copy available from the UCLA Music Library.

Originally for solo piano (*see:* *The Chateau,* W86).

W147. *Anima Divina* (1966) Hollywood

Published by Seesaw Music Corporation. Additional copy available from the UCLA Music Library.

PREMIERE

W147a. 1967 (November 6); University of Arizona College of Fine Arts School of Music; Susann McDonald.

OTHER SELECTED PERFORMANCES

W147b. 1973 (November 18); Santa Barbara; Randall Pratt.

W147c. 1976 (May 3); Carnegie Hall, New York; Randall Pratt.

W147d. 1976 (June 3); Israel.

ORGAN

W148. *Pyramids of Giza* (1971) Hollywood

Unpublished but available from Heroico Music Publications.

Originally for solo piano (*see Egyptian Suite,* W123).

W149. *Saint Francis of Assisi* (1981) Hollywood

Unpublished but available from Heroico Music Publications.

Originally for orchestra (*see:* W17).

STAGE WORKS

W150. *Shepherd in the Distance* (1929) Chicago

Ballet scored for piano. 15 minutes.

Unpublished but available from Heroico Music Publications.

W151. *Wheel of Life* (1933) Chicago

Ballet scored for piano. 15 minutes.

Unpublished but available from Heroico Music Publications.

PREMIERE

W151a. 1933; Chicago, Goodman Theater; Diana Huebert and cast.

W152. *Ubiquity* (Lester Luther) (1937) Chicago and Palo Duro Canyon Studio, Texas

Musical drama scored for SATB/SATB soli and piano. 1 hour.

Unpublished but available from Heroico Music Publications. Additional copy of the score available from the UCLA Music Library.

W153. *Happyland* (Ada Greenfield) (1946) Hollywood

Children's operetta in two acts scored for voices and piano. 1 hour.

Unpublished but available from Heroico Music Publications.

W154. *Red Clay* (1950) Hollywood

Ballet scored for piano. 15 minutes.

Unpublished but available from Heroico Music Publications.

Originally for orchestra (*see:* W22); expanded and arranged for piano.

W155. *Carillon* (Rupert Hughes) (1952) Hollywood

Grand opera in three acts scored for voices and piano. 2 1/2 hours.

Piano-vocal score and parts unpublished but available from Heroico Music Publications.

W156. *The Spider and the Butterfly* (Lena Priscella Hesselberg) (1953) Hollywood

Operetta for children in three acts scored for voices and piano. 45 minutes.

Unpublished but available from Heroico Music Publications. Additional copy of the score available from the UCLA Music Library.

W157. *Kuthara (The Scythe)* (Lester Luther) (1960) Hollywood

Chamber opera in three acts. 1 hour.

Piano-vocal score unpublished but available from Heroico Music Publications. Additional copies of the score available from the American Music Center; UCLA Music Library. Original pencil sketch included in the Moldenhauer Collection, Harvard University.

W157a. 1961 (June 24); Santa Barbara, California. Jack Reed, narrator; Jeanette Farra, dramatic soprano; John Bennett, tenor; Roderick Ristow, baritone; Judith Reed, lyric soprano; Radie Britain, piano and music director. Sponsored by the Santa Barbara chapter of the National Society of Arts and Letters. Directed and produced by Margaret Stromer. *See:* B3, 129, 130, 131.

W158. *The Dark Lady Within* (Shakespeare) (1962) Hollywood

Drama with music scored for piano. 1 hour.

Unpublished but available from Heroico Music Publications.

Commissioned by Marygrove College, Detroit, Michigan.

PREMIERE

W158a. 1962 (May 6); 3 performances in Detroit, Michigan; Sara Lee Stadelman, producer and director. *See:* B9.

W159. *Kambu* (Kate Hammond) (1963) Hollywood

Ballet scored for piano and narrator. 15 minutes.

Unpublished but available from Heroico Music Publications.

W160. *Western Testament* (Sara Lee Stadelman) (1964) Hollywood

Drama with music scored for piano. 1 hour.

Unpublished but available from Heroico Music Publications.

Commissioned by Saint Mary's College, Omaha, Nebraska.

PREMIERE

W160a. 1963 (June 2); TV performance, Omaha, Nebraska. *See:* B9.

OTHER SELECTED PERFORMANCES

W160b. 1964 (June 3, 4, 5); 3 performances, Music Hall, Omaha, Nebraska. Produced and directed by Sara Lee Stadelman.

CHORUS

W161. *Drums of Africa* (R. L. Jenkins) 1934 Chicago

SATB, tom-tom, and piano reduction.

Published by Witmark and Son. Additional copy available from the New York Public Library.

PREMIERE

W161a. 1935 (April 7); Chicago; Chicago Symphonic Choir; Walter Aschenbrenner, conductor. *See:* B64.

W162. *Drums of Africa* (R. L. Jenkins) 1934 Chicago

TTBB.

Published by Witmark and Son.

W163. *Prayer* (Lucille Quarry) 1934 Chicago.

SATB and piano or organ.

Published by Ricordi and Son. Additional copy available from the New York Public Library.

PREMIERE

W163a. 1935 (July 28); New York; Chautauqua Choir; Walter Howe, conductor. *See:* B66.

W164. *Dicky Donkey* (Lester Luther) 1935 Chicago

SATB.

Published by Carl Fischer. Additional copy available from the Texas Composers Collection (University of Texas).

W165. *Dicky Donkey* (Lester Luther) 1935 Chicago

SSAA.

Published by Carl Fischer.

W166. *Fairy of Spring* (Butterfield) 1935 Chicago

SSA.

Published by Heroico Music Publications (first published by Summy Birchard). Additional copy available from the Texas Composers Collection (University of Texas).

W167. *Haunted* (Leo Griffin) 1935 Chicago

SATB.

Unpublished but available from Heroico Music Publications.

W168. *Noontide* (Nietzsche) 1935 Chicago

SSAA.

Published by Heroico Music Publications (first published by Arthur P. Schmidt). Additional copies available from the Amarillo Public Library; American Heritage Center (University of Wyoming); Texas Composers Collection (University of Texas).

First prize, Lake View Musical Society, Chicago, 1936.

W169. *Rain* (Lester Luther) 1935 Chicago

SSA.

Published by Heroico Music Publications (originally published by Arthur P. Schmidt). Additional copies available from the Amarillo Public Library; Texas Composers Collection (University of Texas); Texas Federation of Music Clubs Music Manuscript Archive, Dallas Public Library.

W170. *Baby I Can't Sleep* (folk song) 1936 Chicago

SATB.

Unpublished but available from Heroico Music Publications.

Originally for solo voice (*see:* W222).

First prize, Folk Song contest, Texas Composers' Guild 1936

W171. *Immortality* (Francesco Falk Miller) 1937 Chicago

SATB a cappella.

Published by Arthur P. Schmidt. Additional copy available from the Texas Composers Collection (University of Texas).
PREMIERE

W171a. 1959 (April 10); Chicago; National League of American Pen Women Convention.

W172. *Twilight Moon* (Nelle Eberhart) 1938 Chicago

SSA.

Unpublished but available from Heroico Music Publications.

Originally for solo voice (*see:* W227).

Second National Prize, National League of American Pen Women, 1985.

W173. *Nature Ushers In The Dawn* (Harold Skeath) 1939 Chicago

SATB.

Published by Arthur P. Schmidt. Additional copy available from the Texas Composers Collection (University of Texas).

W174. *The Earth Does Not Wish For Beauty* (Lester Luther) 1940 Chicago

SATB.

Published by Summy Birchard.

Originally for solo voice and piano (*see:* W230).

W175. *I'se Comin' Lord To You* (Alice McKenzie) 1940 Chicago

SATB.

Published by Clayton F. Summy. Additional copies available from the Amarillo Public Library; Texas Composers Collection (University of Texas).

W176. *Lasso Of Time* (Alice McKenzie) 1940 Chicago

TTBB.

Published by Neil Kjos. Additional copy available from the Texas Composers Collection (University of Texas).

Originally for solo voice and piano (*see:* W231).

W177. *Humble Me* (Lester Luther) 1941 Hollywood

SATB.

Unpublished but available from Heroico Music Publications. Additional copy available from the UCLA Music Library.

W178. *Stillness* (Lester Luther) 1941 Hollywood.

SATB.

Published by Heroico Music Publications. Additional copy available from the UCLA Music Library.

Originally for solo voice and piano (*see:* W232).

Selected for symposium held at the University of Texas, Austin, Texas, March 20, 1958.

W179. *Barcarola* (vocalise) 1949 Hollywood

SSAA.

Unpublished but available from Heroico Music Publications.

Originally for violin and piano (*see:* W54).

W180. *The Chalice* (Alma Halff) 1951 Hollywood

SATB.

Unpublished but available from Heroico Music Publications. Additional copy available from the UCLA Music Library.

Originally for voice and piano (*see:* W241).

W181. *The Earth Does Not Wish For Beauty* (Lester Luther) 1953 Hollywood

SATB and Orchestra, 2-2-2-2, 4-3-3, perc., strings. 12 minutes.

Unpublished but available from Heroico Music Publications. Additional copy of the score available from the UCLA Music Library.

Originally for voice and piano (*see:* W230).

W182. *The Star and the Child* (John Lancaster) 1956 Hollywood

SATB.

Published by Heroico Music Publications. Additional copy available from the Texas Federation of Music Clubs Music Manuscript Archive, Dallas Public Library.

PREMIERE

w182a. 1968 (December 17); Santa Monica, CA; *Dolce Spiritoso* Chorus; Eileen McNiece, director.

W183. *The Star and the Child* (John Lancaster) 1956 Hollywood

SSA.

Published by Heroico Music Publications.

W184. *Venete, Felii Audite Me* (Father Fred Cosol) 1957 Hollywood

SSAA.

Unpublished but available from Heroico Music Publications.

W185. *Hush My Heart* (Alma Halff) 1961 Hollywood

SATB.

Unpublished but available from Heroico Music Publications. Additional copy available from the UCLA Music Library.

Originally for solo voice (*see:* W254).

W186. *Hush My Heart* (Alma Halff) 1961 Hollywood

SSAA.

Unpublished but available from Heroico Music Publications. Additional copy available from the UCLA Music Library.

Originally for solo voice (*see:* W254).

W187. *Nisan* (Kate Hammond) 1961 Hollywood

SSAA, piano and string orchestra. 8 minutes.

Published by Heroico Music Publications. Additional copies of the score available from the American Heritage Center (University of Wyoming); Texas Federation of Music Clubs Music Manuscript Archive, Dallas Public Library; UCLA Music Library. Original pencil score included in the Moldenhauer Collection, Harvard University.

First International Award, Delta Omicron International Fraternity, August 21, 1961.

PREMIERE

W187a. 1961 (August 21); Detroit; Detroit Symphony Orchestra and Chorus; Dr. Harry Seitz, conductor.

W188. *Awake to Life* (Lerae Britain) 1963 Hollywood

SATB.

Unpublished but available from Heroico Music Publications. Additional copy available from the UCLA Music Library. Original pencil score included in the Moldenhauer Collection, Harvard University.

PREMIERE

W188a. 1963 (November 2); Whittier, California; Southern California Mormon Choir; Frederick Davis, conductor.

W189. *Harvest Heritage* (Lerae Britain) 1963 Hollywood

SATB.

Unpublished but available from Heroico Music Publications.

Second National Award National League of American Pen Women, 1963.

W190. *Brothers of the Clouds* (Kate Hammond) 1964 Hollywood

TTBB and piano. 8 minutes.

Published by Heroico Music Publications. Additional copies available from the American Music Center; Texas Federation of Music Clubs Music Manuscript Archive, Dallas Public Library.

W191. *Brothers Of The Clouds* (Kate Hammond) 1964 Hollywood

TTBB and orchestra, 2-2-2-2, 4-3-3-1, perc., strings. 10 minutes.

Published by Heroico Music Publications. Score and parts also available from the Fleisher Collection. Additional copies of the score available from the American Heritage Center (University of Wyoming); UCLA Music Library.

Originally for male chorus and piano (*see* : W190).

W192. *Eternal Spirit* (Lerae Britain) 1964 Hollywood

SATB.

Published by Heroico Music Publications.

PREMIERE

W192a. 1971 (May 10); Honolulu, Hawaii; The Church Choir of the Church College of Hawaii; M. Michael Suzuki, conductor.

W193. *The Builders* (Lerae Britain) 1965 Hollywood

SATB and piano.

Published by Heroico Music Publications (originally published by Robert B. Brown). Additional copy available from the Carson County Square House Museum.

W194. *The Flute Song* (Catherine Manore) 1965 Hollywood

SSAA, flute, and piano.

Unpublished but available from Heroico Music Publications. Additional copy available from the American Heritage Center (University of Wyoming).

Commissioned by Sister Marie Constance, IHM and Marygrove College Chorus, Marygrove College, Detroit, Michigan.

W195. *In Silence Of the Temple* (Blanche Collander) 1965 Hollywood

SATB.

Unpublished but available from Heroico Music Publications. Additional copy available from the UCLA Music Library.

W196. *Holy Lullaby* (Alma Halff) 1969 Hollywood

SSA.

Unpublished but available from Heroico Music Publications. Additional copy available from the UCLA Music Library.

Originally for solo voice (*see:* W263).

W197. *Forest Procession* (Lerae Britain) 1970 Hollywood

SATB.

Unpublished but available from Heroico Music Publications. Additional copy available from the UCLA Music Library.

W198. *The Ten Commandments* 1970 Hollywood

SATB and organ.

Unpublished but available from Heroico Music Publications. Additional copies available from the American Heritage Center (University of Wyoming); UCLA Music Library.

W199. *The Builders* (Lerae Britain) 1978 Hollywood

SATB and orchestra, 2-2-2-l, 2-2, timp., perc., strings. 4 minutes.

Unpublished but available from Heroico Music Publications.

Originally for chorus and piano (*see:* W193).

PREMIERE

W199a. 1971 (March 7); Pacific Palisades, California; Brentwood-Westwood Symphony Orchestra; Alvin Mills, conductor; Francis Cain, choral director. *See:* B138.

W200. *Earth Mother* (Radie Britain) 1971 Hollywood

SATB.

Unpublished but available from Heroico Music Publications. Additional copy available from the UCLA Music Library.

W201. *Ka Nani O Ka Lani* (The Beauty of the Heaven) (Lerae Britain) 1971 Hollywood

SATB.

Unpublished but available from Heroico Music Publications.

Originally for solo voice (*see:* W268).

W202. *Little Man* (Mabel Wilton) 1971 Hollywood

SSA.

Unpublished but available from Heroico Music Publications. Additional copy available from the UCLA Music Library.

Originally for solo voice (*see:* W246).

W203. *Song of the Heart* (Lerae Britain) 1971 Hollywood

SATB.

Unpublished but available from Heroico Music Publications.

PREMIERE

W203a. 1971 (April 30); Honolulu, Hawaii; The A Capella Choir of the Church College of Hawaii; M. Michael Suzuki, conductor.

W204. *The Earth Does Not Wish For Beauty* (Lester Luther) (1975) Hollywood

TTBB.

Unpublished but available from Heroico Music Publications. Additional copy available from the UCLA Music Library.

Originally for solo voice and piano (*see:* W230).

Honorable Mention, Intercollegiate Musical Council, Penn State University, June 18, 1976.

W205. *Cherokee Blessing* (Author unknown) 1977 Hollywood

SATB.

Unpublished but available from Heroico Music Publications.

W206. *Lord, God Within Me* (Ernest Holmes) 1977 Hollywood

SATB.

Unpublished but available from Heroico Music Publications.

Additional copy available from the UCLA Music Library.

Originally for solo voice (*see:* W269).

W207. *Lord Have Mercy* 1978 Hollywood

SATB.

Unpublished but available from Heroico Music Publications. Additional copy available from the UCLA Music Library.

W208. *Love Still Has Something Of The Sea* (Sir Charles Sedley) 1980 Hollywood

SATB.

Unpublished but available from Heroico Music Publications. Additional copy available from the UCLA Music Library.

Originally for solo voice (*see:* W247).

W209. *O Sing Unto The Lord* (Psalm 98) 1985 Hollywood

SATB (a cappela).

Unpublished but available from Heroico Music Publications.

SOLO VOICE

[Unless otherwise noted, the following works are scored for voice and piano.]

W210. *Had I A Cave (Liebesleid)* (Robert Burns) 1925 Munich

Originally published by Otto Halbreiter (Munich); later published by Lyon and Healy (Chicago).

PREMIERE

W210a. 1926 (May 4); Munich; Erik Wildhagen, baritone. *See:* B12, 13, 14, 15, 16, 17.

OTHER SELECTED PERFORMANCES

W210b. 1926 (June 5); Starnberg, Germany; Thomas Salcher, tenor. *See:* B18, 19, 20, 24, 36.

W210c. 1927 (February 13); Chicago; Dwight Edrus Cooke, tenor. *See:* B30.

W210d. 1928 (February 10); Amarillo, Texas; Arthur Kraft, tenor. *See:* B49.

W211. *Half Rising Moon* (Banister Tabb) 1925 Munich

Originally published by Otto Halbreiter (Munich); later published by Lyon and Healy (Chicago).

PREMIERE

W211a. 1928 (February 10); Amarillo, Texas; Arthur Kraft, tenor. *See:* B24.

W212. *Immortality (Unsterblichkeit)* (Theodor Storm) 1926 Munich

Unpublished; location of score unknown.

PREMIERE

W212a. 1926 (May 4); Munich; Erik Wildhagen, baritone. *See:* B12, 13, 14, 15, 16, 17.

OTHER SELECTED PERFORMANCES

W212b. 1926 (June 5); Starnberg, Germany; Thomas Salcher, tenor. *See:* B18, 19, 20.

W212c. 1927 (April 11); Dresden, Germany; Erik Wildhagen, baritone. *See:* B32.

W213. *Open The Door To Me (Mach' auf die Tür)* (Robert Burns) 1926 Munich

Originally published by Otto Halbreiter (Munich); later published by Lyon and Healy (Chicago) and Heroico Music Publications. Additional copies available from the Texas Federation of Music Clubs Music Manuscript Archive, Dallas Public Library; UCLA Music Library.

PREMIERE

W213a. 1926 (May 4); Munich; Erik Wildhagen, baritone. *See:* B12, 13, 14, 15, 16, 17, 24, 25.

W213b. 1927 (May 11); Dresden (Germany); Erik Wildhagen, baritone. *See:* B32, 36.

W214. *Sunken City* (Michael Field) Munich 1926

Published by Otto Halbreiter (Munich). Additional copies available from the American Heritage Center (University of Wyoming); Library of Congress; UCLA Music Library.

PREMIERE

W214a. 1926 (June 5); Starnberg, Germany; Thomas Salcher, tenor. *See:* B18, 19, 20.

OTHER SELECTED PERFORMANCES

W214b. 1928 (February 10); Amarillo, Texas; Arthur Kraft, tenor.
W214c. 1928; Munich, Germany; Heinrich Gerfletter, baritone.

W215. *Withered Flowers (Welke Blumen)* (Friedl Schreyvogel) 1926 Munich

Originally published by Otto Halbreiter (Germany); later published by Lyon and Healy (Chicago) and Opus Music Publications. Additional copies available from the Texas Federation of Music Clubs Music Manuscript Archive, Dallas Public Library; UCLA Music Library.

Composers' Press Publication award, 1959.

PREMIERE

W215a. 1926 (May 4); Munich, Germany; Erik Wildhagen, baritone. *See:* B12, 13, 14, 15, 16, 17.

OTHER SELECTED PERFORMANCES

W215b. 1926 (June 5); Starnberg, Germany; Thomas Salcher, tenor. *See:* B18, 19, 20, 28.

W215c. 1927 (April 11); Dresden, Germany; Erik Wildhagen, baritone. *See:* B32, 36.

W216. *Berceuse* (Jean Sanders) 1927 Chicago

Unpublished but available from Heroico Music Publications.

W217. *Hail Texas* (Britain) 1927 Chicago

Published by Gamble Hingle.

Dedicated to Mrs. E. C. Britain.

PREMIERE

W217a. 1927 (January 11); Austin, Texas; May Petersen, soprano. *See:* B31.

W218. *Nirvana* (John Hall Weelock) 1927 Chicago

Originally published by Otto Halbreiter (Munich); later published by Lyon and Healy (Chicago), Robert B. Brown (Hollywood), and Heroico Music Publications. Additional copies available from the Newberry Library (Chicago); Texas Federation of Music Clubs Music Manuscript Archive, Dallas Public Library; UCLA Music LIbrary

First Prize, San Antonio (Texas) Musical Club, 1927. *See:* B33.

PREMIERE

W218a. 1927 (May 11); Dresden, Germany; Erik Wildhagen, baritone. *See:* B32.

OTHER SELECTED PERFORMANCES

W218b. 1927 (October 31); San Antonio, Texas; Mrs. Fred Jones, soprano; Radie Britain, piano. *See:* B37, 38.

W218c. 1927 (December 15); Chicago; Tito Schipa, tenor; Frederick Longas, piano. *See:* B40, 41, 44.

W218d. 1928 (February 10); Amarillo, Texas; Arthur Kraft, tenor. *See:* B49.

W219. *Requiem* (Goethe) 1929 Chicago

Unpublished but available from Heroico Music Publications.

W220. *The Wanderer's Evening Song* (Goethe) 1933 Chicago

Unpublished but available from Heroico Music Publications.

W221. *When We Shall Part* (Mary Stephens Hartley) 1934 Hollywood

Unpublished but available from Heroico Music Publications.

Additional copies available from the American Heritage Center (University of Wyoming); New York Public Library; UCLA Music Library.

W222. *Baby I Can't Sleep* (folk song) 1936 Hollywood

Unpublished but available from Heroico Music Publications.

W223. *Elegy* (Lester Luther) 1937 Chicago

Unpublished but available from Heroico Music Publications. Additional copies available from the New York Public Library; UCLA Music Library.

To Mable Cole.

W224. *In Living Ecstasy* (Harold Skeath) 1938 Chicago

Unpublished but available from Heroico Music Publications. Additional copies available from the UCLA Music Library (two versions: high and low voice).

W225. *In Living Ecstasy* (Harold Skeath) 1938 Chicago

Voice and orchestra.

Unpublished but available from Heroico Music Publications.

Originally for voice and piano (*see :* W224).

PREMIERE

w225a. 1939 (January 26); Chicago; Illinois Symphony Orchestra; Hans Henoit, conductor; Esther Hart, soloist. *See:* B89, 90.

W226. *Sunken City* (Michael Field) 1938 Chicago

Voice and orchestra.

Unpublished but available from Heroico Music Publications.

Originally for voice and piano (*see:* W214).

PREMIERE

w226a. 1939 (January 26); Chicago; Illinois Symphony Orchestra; Hans Henoit, conductor; Esther Hart, soloist. *See:* B89, 90.

W227. *Twilight Moon* (Nelle Eberhart) 1938 Chicago

Unpublished but available from Heroico Music Publications. Additional copies available from the American Heritage Center (University of Wyoming); New York Public Library; UCLA Music Library.

W228. *Twilight Moon* (Nelle Eberhart) 1938 Chicago

Voice and orchestra.

Unpublished but available from Heroico Music Publications.

Originally for voice and piano (*see:* W227).

PREMIERE

W228a. 1939 (January 26); Chicago; Illinois Symphony Orchestra; Hans Henoit, conductor; Esther Hart, soloist. *See:* B89, 90.

W229. *Open The Door To Me* (Robert Burns) 1939 Munich

Voice and orchestra.

Unpublished but available from Heroico Music Publications.

Originally for voice and piano (*see:* W213).

PREMIERE

W229a. 1939 (January 26); Chicago; Illinois Symphony Orchestra; Hans Heniot, conductor; Esther Hart, soloist. *See:* B89, 90.

W230. *The Earth Does Not Wish For Beauty* (Lester Luther) 1940 Chicago

Unpublished but available from Heroico Music Publications. Additional copy available from the UCLA Music Library.

W231. *Lasso of Time* (Alice McKenzie) 1940 Chicago

Originally published by Neil Kjos (Chicago); later published by Heroico Music Publications. Additional copies available from the Carson County Square House Museum; New York Public Library; UCLA Music Library.

"Lovingly dedicated to my mother and father."

See: B108.

W232. *Stillness* (Lester Luther) 1940 Chicago

Unpublished but available from Heroico Music Publications. Additional copies available from the New York Public Library; UCLA Music Library.

W233. *Life's Ebb and Flow* (Elsie M. Fowler) 1941 Hollywood

Unpublished but available from Heroico Music Publications. Additional copy available from the New York Public Library.

W234. *Eternal Cycle* (Alta Turk Everett) 1942 Hollywood

Unpublished but available from Heroico Music Publications.

W235. *Love Me Today* (Isabel Dewett) 1942 Hollywood

Unpublished but available from Heroico Music Publications. Additional copies available from the Library of Congress; New York Public Library; UCLA Music Library.

W236. *Serenade* (Isabel Dewett) 1942 Hollywood

Unpublished but available from Heroico Music Publications.

W237. *Silver Wings* (John G. Magee) 1942 Hollywood

Unpublished but available from Heroico Music Publications. Additional copy available from the Amarillo Public Library.

W238. *All Alone on the Prairie* (Radie Britain) 1945 Hollywood

Unpublished but available from Heroico Music Publications.

W239. *More Rain, More Rest* (author unknown) 1945 Hollywood

Unpublished but available from Heroico Music Publications.

W240. *Love Song of the Taj Mahal* (Alma Halff) 1947 Hollywood

For harp and narrator.

Unpublished but available from Heroico Music Publications. Additional copies available from the American Heritage Center (University of Wyoming); UCLA Music Library.

W240a. 1948 (June 3); Los Angeles; Roberta Blackstone Smith, narrator.

W241. *The Chalice* (Alma Halff) 1948 Hollywood

Unpublished but available from Heroico Music Publications. Additional copies available from the Amarillo Public Library; American Heritage Center (University of Wyoming); UCLA Music Library.

Second prize, Texas Federation of Music Clubs, 1952.

W242. *Goddess of Inspiration* (Paramanda) 1948 Hollywood

Unpublished but available from Heroico Music Publications.

W243. *Vision of Loveliness* (Ada Greenfield) 1948 Hollywood

Unpublished but available from Heroico Music Publications.

W244. *Farewell At Dawn* (Rupert Hughes) 1949 Hollywood

Unpublished but available from Heroico Music Publications. Additional copy available from the American Heritage Center (University of Wyoming).

W245. *Your Hand* (Mary Miller Beard) 1949 Hollywood

Unpublished but available from Heroico Music Publications.

W246. *Little Man* (Mabel Wilton) 1951 Hollywood

Unpublished but available from Heroico Music Publications. Additional copies available from the New York Public Library; UCLA Music Library.

W247. *Love Still Has Something Of the Sea* (Sir Charles Sedley) 1952 Hollywood

Unpublished but available from Heroico Music Publications. Additional copies available from the American Heritage Center (University of Wyoming); UCLA Music Library.

To Gertrude and Frank Viault.

W248. *Soil Magic* (Genoa Morris) 1955 Hollywood

Unpublished but available from Heroico Music Publications.

W249. *Revelation* (Lester Luther) 1958 Hollywood

Unpublished but available from Heroico Music Publications. Additional copy available from the UCLA Music Library.

W250. *Voudoun* (Kate Hammond) 1958 Hollywood

Unpublished but available from Heroico Music Publications.

W251. *From Far Away* (Katherine Bainbridge) 1960 Hollywood

Unpublished but available from Heroico Music Publications. Additional copy available from the UCLA Music Library.

W252. *Old Black Levee* (Kate Hammond) 1960 Hollywood

Unpublished but available from Heroico Music Publications.

W253. *Barcarola* (vocalise) 1961 Hollywood

Published by Ossian Music Publisher (Paris) and Heroico Music Publications. Additional copies available from the Texas Federation of Music Clubs Music Manuscript Archive, Dallas Public Library; UCLA Music Library.

Originally for violin and piano (*see:* W54).

W254. *Hush My Heart* (Alma Halff) 1961 Hollywood

Published by Heroico Music Publications. Additional copies available from the Carson County Square House Museum; Texas Federation of Music Clubs Music Manuscript Archive, Dallas Public Library; UCLA Music Library.

W255. *You* (Elvina McNary) 1961 Hollywood

Published by Heroico Music Publications. Additional copies available from the American Music Center; Carson County Square House Museum; Texas Federation of Music Clubs Music Manuscript Archive, Dallas Public Library; UCLA Music Library.

W256. *The Secret* (Ralph S. Cushman) 1962 Hollywood

Unpublished but available from Heroico Music Publications.

W257. *Eternal Spirit* (Lerae Britain) 1964 Hollywood

Unpublished but available from Heroico Music Publications. Additional copy available from the UCLA Music Library.

Originally for chorus (*see:* W192).

W258. *Lullaby of the Bells* (Aileen Caryle) 1964 Hollywood

Published by Heroico Music Publications. Additional copies available from the Texas Federation of Music Clubs Music Manuscript Archive, Dallas Public Library; UCLA Music Library. Original sketches included in the Moldenhauer Collection, Harvard University.

W259. *The Builders* (Lerae Britain) 1965 Hollywood

Published by Heroico Music Publications.

Originally for chorus and piano (*see:* W193).

W260. *Casa Blanca By The Sea* (Elvina McNary) 1967 Hollywood

Unpublished but available from Heroico Music Publications. Additional copies available from the American Heritage Center (University of Wyoming); UCLA Music Library.

First Prize National League of American Pen Women, 1970.

W261. *Elvina de la Luz* (Ellen Wood) 1967 Hollywood

Published by Heroico Music Publications. Additional copies available from the American Heritage Center (University of Wyoming); UCLA Music Library.

"Humbly and in admiring remembrance."

W262. *Have I Told You* (Lerae Britain) 1967 Hollywood

Unpublished but available from Heroico Music Publications.

W263. *Holy Lullaby* (Alma Halff) 1969 Hollywood

Unpublished but available from Heroico Music Publications. Additional copy available from the UCLA Music Library.

W264. *Overtones* (William Alexander Percy) 1970 Hollywood

Solo voice and flute.

Unpublished but available from Heroico Music Publications. Additional copy available from the UCLA Music Library.

PREMIERE

W264a. 1975 (October 18); Los Angeles; June Montgomery, soprano, Elise Moennig, flute.

W265. *Translunar Cycle* **(Spacewalk, Moonscape, Earthrise)** (Kate Hammond) 1970 Hollywood

Unpublished but available from Heroico Music Publications.

W266. *Earth Mother* (Radie Britain) 1971 Hollywood

Unpublished but available from Heroico Music Publications. Additional copies available from the American Heritage Center (University of Wyoming); UCLA Music Library.

Originally for chorus (*see:* W199).

W267. *Ka Nani O Ka Lani* **(The Beauty of the Heaven)** (Lerae Britain) 1971 Hollywood

Unpublished but available from Heroico Music Publications.

W268. *Lord, God Within Me* (Ernest Holmes) 1971 Hollywood

Unpublished but available from Heroico Music Publications. Additional copies available from the American Heritage Center (University of Wyoming); UCLA Music Library.

W269. *My Dream* (Allen Ezell) 1971 Hollywood

Unpublished but available from Heroico Music Publications.

W270. *A Tribute* (Alma Halff) 1971 Hollywood

Published by Heroico Music Publications.

OTHER SELECTED PERFORMANCES

W270a. 1989 (spring); Manila, Philippines; Lucretia Shaw, soprano.

W271. *Lotusland* (Elvina McNary) 1972 Hollywood

Published by Heroico Music Publications. Additional copy available from the UCLA Music Library.

W272. *Song Of The Heart* (Lerae Britain) 1972 Hollywood

Unpublished but available from Heroico Music Publications. Additional copies available from the American Heritage Center (University of Wyoming); UCLA Music Library.

Originally for chorus (*see:* W202).

The Earth Does Not Wish For Beauty [voice and brass ensemble] 1975. *See:* W68.

W273. *Love Song* (Ann Marx) 1978 Hollywood

Unpublished but available from Heroico Music Publications.

W274. *Weep Not* (Alma Halff) 1979 Hollywoood

Unpublished but available from Heroico Music Publications. Additional copy available from the UCLA Music Library.

W275. *Fulfillment* (Helen L. Cassidy) 1980 Hollywood

Unpublished but available from Heroico Music Publications. Additional copy available from the UCLA Music Library.

W276. *I Found A Star* (Frances Grant Nachant) 1980 Hollywood

Unpublished but available from Heroico Music Publications. Additional copy available from the UCLA Music Library.

W277. *We Are The Wind Chimes* (Bonnie M. Pratt) 1981 Hollywood

Unpublished but available from Heroico Music Publications.

W278. *Lost River* (Helen L. Cassidy) 1982 Hollywood

Unpublished but available from Heroico Music Publications.

W279. *Mother (A Melody of Love)* (Radie Britain) 1982 Hollywood

Narrator and piano.

Unpublished but available from Heroico Music Publications.

W280. *Mother (A Melody of Love)* (Radie Britain) 1982 Hollywood

Voice and orchestra, 2-2-2-2, 2-2-2-0, timp., strings, harp and narrator. 9 minutes.

Unpublished but available from Heroico Music Publications.

Originally for narrator and piano (*see:* W279).

Bibliography

A CHRONOLOGICAL LIST OF WRITINGS BY RADIE BRITAIN

B1. "A Composer Looks at American Music." *Pan Pipes*, 1946. Reprint: *Music of the West Magazine* (September 1955); *Amarillo Globe-Times* (Fall 1955).

Observations on the state of American music and expressions of concern about the prevalance of popular music, the inaccessibility of new orchestral scores to conductors, the belief that the music of New York, "a cosmopolitan city of the world," can express "the emotions of the American people," and the tendencies of composers to build "names" and judge merit on the basis of "copies sold" rather than on "genuine artistic merit." "American composers need to live over our soil."

B2. *Bravo*, unpublished autobiographical novel. 1959

Account of Miss Britain's relationship with Edgardo Simone.

B3. "Radie Britain Expresses View on Composition of New Opera." Interview with Smith Russell, *Music of the West Magazine* 16 (August 1961): 4.

Interview concerning the composition of *Kuthara (see:* W157) which reveals Miss Britain's thoughts about modern music. "Q. How do you classify *Kuthara* musically? A. I have mingled contemporary and melodic styles—and it would not surprise me to be criticised for that—but I used harsh dissonances to emphasize the conflicts in the development of the drama and melodies to enhance the love interest and the more harmonious relationships. Q. Is that bad? A. I am sure that most of us like to hear melody and I am very sure that singers like to sing melodies, but melodic writing seems to be old-fashioned. Q. Do you mean that contemporary music cannot have any melody and that any music which has melodies cannot, therefore, be 'contemporary'? A. No, but it should have logic and beauty. . . . My firm belief is that good music of any age must come from the heart rather than just the mind. In other words, the emotional content is the most important; but that requires a scholarly technique to express it properly. Q. Then do you consider yourself a composer of what is called 'contemporary' music? A. I use modern harmonies, but with strong melodic lines above them."

B4. *Major and Minor Moods.* Hollywood, California: Heroico Music Publications, 1970.

A collection of autobiographical and inspirational short stories.

B5. "Musical Composition: A New World for Women." *The Instrumentalist* 25/4 (November 1970): 55-56.

Brief historical synopsis of the place of women in music, focussing on the traditional repression of women musicians and citing such successful women as the conductors Antonia Brico and Ethel Leginska. "At this point in history, I have found the life of a woman composer to be highly rewarding and satisfying, but the woman's role in the field of musical composition is just beginning to emerge. We need continued exposure of our works and conductors who are not prejudiced."

B6. *Composer's Corner.* Hollywood, California: Highland Music Company, 1978.

Collection of musical articles from *National Pen Women Magazine* detailing all aspects of musical experience and the creative process, with copious quotations from a variety of musical and philosophical sources. *See:* B143, 144.

B7. "Talk at Brentwood/Westwood Symphony Presentation," the author's handwritten notes, Los Angeles, September 9, 1979.

Ideas on creativity. "A composer must give of himself. This is true of any artist, but it seems more of a creative musician. When we listen to a composer's creation, we listen to his individual personality, and if we write music of any value, we must know how to express ourselves in tones. I have heard it said that the first phrase a person utters discloses his culture and refinement. So I believe it is with music. The depth or height one can reach is the depth or height of his creation. For I believe music is a higher revelation than philosophy. It is said that modern civilization has ceased to develop its intuitive powers. If that is true of a creative artist, creation in his soul has ceased for intuitive power should be developed into the highest form. And a composer must have sufficient technique to free his inspiration to be able to put his highest thoughts into tones. . . . One writes rapidly to catch these immortal glimpses of inspiration, feeling the mood of perfection at the time, then, when the work is cold, the analytical mind takes over, and practically before the work is completed, new melodies are forming. . . . I feel a composer should compose as if he were going to die at the end of each composition. Then, only then, will the greatest sincerity evolve—the true nobility being superior to one's former self. . . . On my piano I keep these inspired lines:

> Think noble thoughts,
> Dream beautiful dreams,
> Labor constructively from day to day,
> And when one is ready for a greater accomplishment
> The work one is to do will come to hand.
> The universe always has work for those who are qualified to create it."

B8. *Ridin' Herd to Writing Symphonies: The Autobiography of Radie Britain*, unpublished, 1980.

A lengthy, engaging memoire of Miss Britain's life and musical experiences. Currently unpublished, it is being considered for publication by a number of university presses.

B9. "Reflections," the author's undated handwritten notes.

Thoughts on the creation of *Western Testatment* and *The Dark Lady Within* with general observations on musical creation. "One must have a plan and a stimulation in forming musical thought patterns—a perspective and a flaming desire to concentrate and permit the golden thread of inspiration to flow through one's phantasy." *See:* W160 and W158.

B10. "Talk Given at SAI Convention," the author's undated handwritten notes.

Biographical sketch and thoughts on the creative process. "The greatest satisfaction in a composer's life is the conception of a composition: discovering a melody out of thin air and capturing its quality hurriedly on paper—not to lose its magic. Many times our phantasy exceeds our actual ability to put into form what we have heard. Perhaps that is why we continue to write—hoping the perfect work will appear on paper. . . . It is a constant growing process, gaining sufficient technique to weave a melody into any mood or pattern that we desire—realizing that we are absorbing stardust that we are a part of. . . . Early in my career I felt I must dip my pen into my arteries and write—trusting the invisible would take fruition with an honest and inspired work with no padding, but every measure must sing from the heart. The composer must have sufficient technique to be flexible with any idea that is worthy of a musical treatment. It is a good plan to try the melody with many variations and over a multitude of dynamic rhythms to see if it has adequate possibilities for extended forms. In fact the composer must strike the strings of his heart with fire! A creator must dissolve himself into the universe and feel the touch of the Divine as he bestows his gift of creativity through Him. For I feel the musical soul is placed in the body like a diamond and it must be polished and polished or the lustre will fade. . . . I believe we are reeds through which He blows His melody and we must be very sensitive to receive these musical melodies for the human soul is a dynamo generating a spiritual electricity from a magnetic field as vast as the universe."

A CHRONOLOGICAL LIST OF WRITINGS ABOUT RADIE BRITAIN AND HER MUSIC

1926-1928

B11. "Texas Composers to Be Heard in Dallas Concert." *Dallas Morning News*, May 2, 1926, section 3, p. 1.

Announcement of the upcoming concert of Texas composers' music sponsored by the Dallas Music Teachers' Association. "Songs by Miss Radie Britain also will be heard. Miss Britain hails from Amarillo, but at present is concertizing in Germany. Her songs have enjoyed more than conventional success abroad."

B12. "Münchener Konzerte." *Münchener Post*, May 14, 1926.

Review of four songs performed by Erik Wildhagen, baritone, in Munich, May 4, 1926. The songs are "proof of a subtle and sensitive musician, in a personally-distinctive, moderately modern harmonic language."

["... eine Uraufführung: vier Lieder von Radie Britain, mit der Komponistin am Flügel. Es sind Zeugnisse einer feingebildeten und feinempfindenden Musikerin, in der harmonischen Sprache gemäßigt modern, doch reizvolle persönliche Züge aufweisend. Die Wirkung der in ziemlich gleichem Stil und Stimmung gehaltenen Lieder—'Liebesleid', 'Mach' auf die Tür', 'Welke Blumen', 'Unsterblichkeit'—beschränkt sich auf das Intime, doch steht zu erwarten, daß die noch junge, zweifellos sehr begabte Tonsetzerin sich auch zur bedeutenden Gestalterin entwickeln wird." *See:* W210a, W212a, W213a, and W215a.

B13. Gerheuser, Dr. G. *Münchener Zeitung,* May 17, 1926.

Review of four songs performed by Erik Wildhagen, baritone, in Munich, May 4, 1926. "Three [sic] songs by Radie Britain were premiered with the composer herself accompanying on the piano. This young lady already shows an amazing talent for rendering poetic texts correctly in music. She has a feeling for melodic line and logical form. The limits of her interesting harmonies are widely set, in the modern style. Temperament and passionate feeling motivate her musical expression. If the expressive texts which she has set to music are not exhausted of their deepest meaning, we will not hold this against her, and Radie Britain may be comforted with the thought that Beethoven and Wagner, at the same age, could not have done better."

["In Uraufführung wurden gesungen drei Lieder von Radie Britain, deren Begleitung die Komponistin am Flügel selbst besorgte. Die junge Dame zeigt schon ein erstaunliches Talent, das Dichterwort musikalisch zutreffend wiederzugeben, sie hat Sinn für melodische Linie und logische Formgestaltung; die Grenzen ihrer interessanten Harmonik sind neuzeitlich weit gesteckt, Temperament und leidenschaftliches Fühlen beflügeln ihre musikalische Ausdrucksweise. Wenn die anspruchsvollen Texte, die sie sich zur Vertonung gewählt hatte, nicht voll in ihrem tiefsten Inhalte ausgeschöpft waren, so wollen wir dies nicht weiter schlimm anrechnen, und Radie Britain mag sich mit dem Gedanken trösten, daß auch Beethoven und Wagner im gleichen Alter das noch nicht gekonnt haben."] *See:* W210a, W212a, W213a, and W215a.

B14. "Münchener Konzerte." *Allgemeine Zeitung,* Nr. 112, May 18, 1926.

Review of four songs performed by Erik Wildhagen, baritone, in Munich, May 4, 1926. "The composer was given a friendly reception."

["Das Programm brachte schließlich die Uraufführung einiger Lieder von Radie Britain. Es sind wohlgestaltete, aus der Erfühlung des dichterischen Stimmungscharakters stammende Arbeiten in fesselnder harmonischer Beleuchtung, die der am Flügel begleitenden Komponistin einen freundlichen Erfolg eintrugen."] *See:* W210a, W212a, W213a, and W215a.

B15. Z., Dr. W. *Münchner Tagblatt*, Nr. 139, May 20, 1926.

Review of four songs performed by Erik Wildhagen, baritone, in Munich, May 4, 1926. Miss Britain is labeled a "promising talent."

["Dank muß man Erik Wildhagen auch dafür wissen, daß er sich mit erfolggekröntem Gelingen für das Schaffen einer jungen Komponistin und Schülerin Albert Noeltes einsetzte, Radie Britain. Die Uraufführung der vier Lieder auf Texte von Robert Burns, Friedl Schreyvogel (bei der mich nur das entsetzlich schiefe Bild störte, daß 'ein Duften aus dem Glase steigt, wie Menschen grüßen!') und Theodor Storm machte mit einem verheißungsvollen Talente bekannt. Freilich, "kein Meister fällt vom Himmel, auch keine Meisterin," deshalb konnte ein Lied, wie das in seinen Stimmungen wechselnde "Mach auf die Tür" trotz fesselnder Einzelheiten noch nicht ganz bewältigt und gestaltet werden, dafür aber zeugten "Welke Blumen" und das Stormische "Wer je gelebt in Liebesarmen" in ihrem einheitlicheren Stimmungsgehalt ein feines Ein- und Durchführungsvermögen und die Kraft zu selbständiger Verlautbarung der so erfaßten Gefühlskomplexe. Der Komponistin, die selbst am Flügle saß, während die anderen Lieder von Franz Hallasch gediegen begleitet wurden, sowie ihrem hingebungsvollen Interpreten wurde verdienter, sehr herzlicher Beifall zuteil."] *See:* W210a, W212a, W213a, and W215a.

B16. Ru., H. *Münchner Neueste Nachrichten*, Nr. 128, [May 1926].

Review of four songs performed by Erik Wildhagen, baritone, in Munich, May 4, 1926. "The four songs of Radie Britain, which, with the composer as first-rate accompanist, were premiered with great success that evening, proved that it was only a knowing, guiding hand that was needed to put the singer on the right path to song. They demonstrate a sense of melody as noble as it is strongly expressive, which, in combination with the harmonically rich accompaniment, hit upon the atmosphere and emotional contents of the poems and, in part, really deepened them. The creative powers were most impressive and unified in "Liebesleid" and especially in "Welke Blumen," while they were not entirely sufficient in "Mach' auf die Tur" and "Unsterblichkeit."

["Daß es übrigens nur der verständnisvoll führenden Hand bedürfte, um ihn auch dem Lied gegenüber auf den rechten Weg zu bringen, bewiesen die vier Lieder von Radie Britain, die mit der Komponistin als trefflicher Begleiterin außerdem an dem Abend zur Uraufführung kamen und viel Erfolg hatten. Sie zeigen Sinn für eine ebenso edle wie ausdruckskräftige Melodik, die in Verbindung mit der harmonisch reich bedachten Begleitung den Stimmungs- und Empfindungsgehalt der Dichtungen gut trifft und teilweise wesentlich vertieft. Am eindrucksvollsten und zugleich fein geschlossene Liedgebilde schaffend ist dies gelungen in Liebesleid und besonders in Welke Blumen, während für Mach' auf die Tür und Unsterblichkeit die Gestaltungskraft doch nicht ganz ausreichte."] *See:* W210a, W212a, W213a, and W215a.

B17. St., H. *München-Augesburger Abendzeitung,* [May 1926].

Review of four songs performed by Erik Wildhagen, baritone, in Munich, May 4, 1926. "From all four songs speaks a deep understanding of poetic content, lyrical sensitivity, sense of melodic line, and, above all, a harmonic sensitiveness inspired by interesting and distinctive turns of phrase. So, for instance, there is something which thrills of pain and lamentation in the sensitive harmonic coloring of Burns' 'Had I a Cave,' which, according to my mind, is the most perfect of the four songs in regard to form and content. 'Open the Door', the poem also by Burns, begins with a most fascinating accompanying figure. The uncommonly clever and difficult musical setting of the constantly returning exclamation 'O' would alone be sufficient to call serious attention to this young composer."

["Die Pianistin Radie Britain stellte sich in einem Konzert des Baritonisten Erik Wildhagen auch als Komponistin vor, und zwar mit vier Liedern, die sie selbst feinsinnig und mit kultivierter Technik am Flügel begleitete. Aus allen vier spricht Verständnis für den poetischen Gehalt, lyrisches Empfinden, Sinn für die melodische Linie und vor allem eine harmonische Empfindsamkeit, die zu interessantesten und scharf charakterisierenden Wendungen inspiriert. So schwingt etwas Packendes von Schmerz und Klage in der harmonischen Färbung des Burnsschen Gedichtes "Liebesleid," das nach Form und musikalischem Inhalt mir als das geglückteste erscheint. Das zweite, ebenfalls von Burns, beginnt, auch in der Begleitungsfigur, ungemein reizvoll, zerfließt allerdings etwas gegen das Ende zu. Aber wenn es nur die außerordentlich geschickte (und gewiß ebenso schwierige) Vertonung des immer wiederkehrenden Ausrufs "Oh!" wäre, so würde es genügen, die Aufmerksamkeit auf das ausgesprochene Talent der jungen Komponistin zu lenken. "Welke Blumen" ist etwas konventioneller geraten, "Unsterblichkeit" (nach Storm) sehr geschlossen und wirkungsvoll. Überall ist der Stimme eine dankbarer Aufgabe gestellt."] *See:* W210a, W212a, W213a, and W215a.

B18. [Starnberg, Germany, June 1926]

> Review of four songs performed by Thomas Salcher, tenor, and
> Franz Hallasch, pianist in Starnberg, Germany, June 5, 1926.
> The songs were labeled the "artistic highpoint" of the program,
> and were said to embody "an unusually sensitive, highly culti-
> vated artistic soul."

> ["Einen künstlerischen Höhepunkt im engeren Sinne bildete die
> Erstaufführung von vier Tenorliedern der genial begabten
> jungen amerikanischen Komponistin Radie Britain (einer
> Schülerin des einheimischen Komponisten Albert Noelte):
> "Liebesleid," "Die versunkene Stadt," "Welke Blumen" und
> "Unsterblichkeit." Aus diesen Liedern spricht eine ungemein
> zartbesaitete, hochkultivierte Künstlerseele, deren äußerst
> sensible, melodische und ungewöhnlich interessante harmoni-
> sche Ausdrucksweise den verschiedenen Stimmungsphasen der
> mit feinem Geschmack gewählten Gedichte in meisterhafter
> Weise gerecht wird. Besonders "Die versunkene Stadt" zeigte
> eine Tiefe und Schönheit des Ausdrucks, der dieses Lied neben
> den schönsten Eingebungen großer Liedmeister würdig bestehen
> läßt: den unmittelbarsten Erfolg hatte "Welke Blumen" (das
> wiederholt werden mußte) dank seiner ungemein eindringlichen
> und wirkungsvollen Melodik."] *See:* W210b, W212b, W214a,
> and W215b.

B19. [Starnberg, Germany, June 1926]

> Review of four songs performed by Thomas Salcher, tenor, and
> Franz Hallasch, pianist in Starnberg, Germany, June 5, 1926.
> "Proof of an unusually large talent. . . ."

> ["Solist des Abends ist Thomas Salcher, der vier Lieder von
> Radie Britain, einer genial begabten jungen amerikanischen
> Komponistin (Schülerin von Albert Noelte) mit Kapellmeister Dr.
> Franz Hallasch vom Nationaltheater in München am Flügel, zur
> Aufführung bringen wird. Diese Lieder, Zeugnisse einer
> ungewöhnlich grossen Begabung, erzielten jüngst in einem
> Konzert in München sensationellen Erfolg bei Publikum und
> Presse."] *See:* W210b, W212b, W214a, and W215b.

B20. [Starnberg, Germany, June 1926]

> Review of four songs performed by Thomas Salcher, tenor, and
> Franz Hallasch, pianist in Starnberg, Germany, June 5, 1926.
> "Very interesting songs by the composer Radie Britain, an ex-
> traordinarily talented young student of Albert Noelte—songs of
> singular harmonic and melodic charm. . . ."

["Solist des Abends war unser Landsmann Thomas Salcher, dessen Qualität als stimmbegabter, musikalischer und intelligenter Sänger an dieser Stelle schon öfters rühmend erwähnt wurde. Hochinteressant waren die von ihm zum Vortrag gewählten Lieder der Komponistin Radie Britain, einer außerordentlich begabten jungen Schülerin von A. Nölte—Lieder von harmonisch und melodisch reizvoller Eigenart, in denen die Stimmung der zur Vertonung außerordentlich geeigneten Dichtungen voll zum Ausdruck kam, in der "Versunkenen Stadt" die grenzenlos traurige Öde, wie sie das Gedicht vermittelt. "Liebesleid" hat etwas unmittelbar Packendes in seiner düsteren Stimmung, "Welke Blumen" appelieren mit zarter einschmeichelnder Lyrik direkt an Ohr und Gemüt. "Unsterblichkeit," ein mit leidenschaftlichem Impuls gestaltetes Schlußlied, erzielte schon in Folge der effektvollen stimmlichen Behandlung tiefe Wirkung. Salcher war vorzüglicher Interpret der Lieder. Am Flügel war dem Sänger Kapellmeister Dr. Hallasch trefflicher Begleiter."] *See:* W210b, W212b, W214a, and W215b.

B21. "Albert Noelte Here on a Visit." *Musical Courier* 93/7 (August 12, 1926): 13.

Short biographical sketch of Noelte with reference to his "advanced pupil in composition Radie Britain." "A number of Miss Britain's compositions have been issued by established German publishers, and Mr. Noelte regards her as having most unusual talent."

B22. "Albert Noelte in America on a Visit." [August 1926?]

Short notice that Noelte's visit to the United States has included coaching American students, "among them Radie Britain, a Texas girl [with] very unusual talent [and] a remarkable reputation as a writer of music."

B23. "The Compositions of Radie Britain." *Musical Courier* 93/11 (September 9, 1926): 23.

Brief recounting of Radie Britain's origins in Texas, her recent studies abroad, and her presence in Chicago to continue her studies with Noelte. "Miss Britain intends to make composition her life work, and she has met with considerable success abroad."

B24. "Radie Britain Here." *Musical Courier* 93/12 (September 16, 1926): 20.

Short article notes Radie Britain's presence in Chicago and announces that her publications ("Open the Door to Me," "Half

Rising Moon," "Had I A Cave," Prelude, *Western Suite)* are being displayed in the show windows of two local music firms. *See:* W213a, W211a, W210b, W82a, and W83a.

B25. "Radie Britain Publishes New Suite for Piano." [Amarillo, September 1926?]

Announcement that the recently published *Western Suite* and "Open the Door To Me" are now available in Amarillo. "Miss Britain is already recognized by eminent musicians and critics as an original and rarely endowed musician whos [*sic*] works promise added importance to American music literature." *See:* W83a and W213a.

B26. B. "Radie Britain's Chicago Debut." *Music News* (Chicago), December 10, 1926.

Review of Miss Britain's performance of her *Western Suite* and Prelude in G-flat for piano at the South Shore Country Club. "Radie Britain, who is rapidly gaining recognition as a composer of unusual talent and originality, introduced . . . her *Western Suite* for piano. In this work, according to my knowledge, the first attempt has been made to convey a specific and typical American atmosphere, one livid [sic] with unsentimental romance, dignity, vastness and vitality, . . . within the boundaries of absolute music. . . . Althoughly decidedly modern in its melodic outline and remarkably colorful harmonic background, this music never stoops to the mean devices of cacaphoneous or rhythmic distortions. It is logical throughout in form as well as in its harmonic development, it is full of vitality, healthy emotion and the effervescence of a truly musical and artistic personality. . . . The young composer . . . and her work were the objects of a most hearty ovation at the end of the performance." An encore, the Prelude in G-flat, is "a piece of classic design and noble expressiveness that fully deserves to be ranked with the best of American standard piano literature." *See:* W82a and W83a.

B27. "Introducing Radie Britain." *Musical Courier* 93/25 (December 16, 1926): 10.

Glowing article including a review of Britain's Chicago debut at the South Shore Country Club (playing the *Western Suite* and Prelude) and a detailed discussion of her training and her recent compositional successes. "Brief introductory remarks acquainted the audience with the deeper programmatic purport of her work *[Western Suite]*, which, however, borders the realm of musical realism only accidentally . . . , the total contents impressing in fact as absolute music of an unusually high artistic standard. The vitality which pulsates through Radie Britain's music is astounding. Here is indeed a high and unsophisticated talent pouring forth heartfelt sounds with the enthusiasm of the believer in the beautiful and sublime in music. Yet her mode of musical expression is governed by a keen sense for logic and insistency in form and harmony. True, a dominating key as fixed purpose is hardly discernible, but the iridescent harmonies blend perfectly, forming a most striking background for sweeping and strongly accentuated melodic lines of sensuous beauty and strong impressiveness. . . . But perhaps the outstanding feature at a first hearing of this work is its lack of what is generally termed feminine timidity; though a certain air of refined modesty in the manner of emotional expression is evident—a reserve inherent with highly strung, sensitive creative artists—this music is alive with vitality and with the fervor of sincere and convincing ardency." *See:* W82a and W83a.

B28. "A New Radie Britain Song." *Musical Courier* 94/3 (January 20, 1927): 9.

Brief announcement of the publication of "Withered Flowers," opus 6, by Halbreiter in Munich with translated selections from unspecified German reviews. ". . . wonderfully impressive and highly effective melodic line." ". . . tender ingratiating melody [appealed] directly to the ear as well as to the heart." ". . . an equally noble and refined, and strongly expressive melodic line, which in connection with uncommonly rich harmonic background not only adequately but really deepens the atmosphere and emotional contents of the poem." *See:* W215b.

B29. "Radie Britain's Composition on Alma Mehus' Programs." *Musical Courier* 94/4 (January 27, 1927): 8.

Very brief note concerning the inclusion of "The Covered Wagon" from *Western Suite* on pianist Alma Mehus' concert-tour programs. *See:* W83a.

B30. W., C. E.. "Galajikian-Cooke-Brittain [sic]-Girvin." *The Music News* (Chicago), February 18, 1927.

Review of a recital by "Dwight Edrus Cooke, tenor, Florence Galajikian, pianist-composer-accompanist, and Radie Britain, composer-accompanist" at the studios of the Girvin Institute of Musical Arts in Chicago that included Britain's "Had I a Cave." Britain's songs displayed "strong impulse, splendid scoring in the piano accompaniments . . . , and with a vocal line of extreme beauty." They are of "extreme modernity but are clear-cut and truly logical in build." *See:* W210c.

B31. "May Peterson Dedicates New Texas Song, 'Hail Texas,' At Inauguration of Dan Moody as Governor of Texas." *Musical Courier* 94/
12, (March 24, 1927): 47.

Large photo of inauguration with lengthy caption identifying the
people in the photo. "May Peterson sang "Hail Texas" just before
Governor Moody took the oath of office. The song was written by
Radie Britain of Amarillo, Texas." *See:* W217a.

B32. "Radie Britain's Songs in Dresden." *Musical Courier* 94/17 (April 28,
1927): 41.

Brief note of the performance of "Withered Flowers," "Open the
Door to Me," "Immortality," and "Nirvana" on April 11th in Dres-
den by Erik Wildhagen, leading baritone of the Munich Grand
Opera. *See:* W215c, W213b, W212c, and W218a.

B33. "Radie Britain's Song Takes First Prize," *Musical Courier* 94/21 (May
26, 1927): 40.

Brief report of the first prize taken by "Nirvana" in the song
contest of the San Antonio Musical Club, and an announcement
that Britain would be conducting classes in piano and composition in Amarillo during June and July. *See:* W218.

B34. "Praise for Radie Britain Compositions." [May 1927?]

Short reference to reception of the songs composed in Munich.
"The Dallas, Tex., *Musicale* of recent date published the following words of praise for the compositions of Radie Britain, gifted
American composer: 'Another Texan has achieved notable recognition in European and American musical circles in the person of Radie Britain. A musician's review of Miss Britain's
compositions gives them most favorable comment, saying they
are very original, rather modern and indicative of a highly developed musicianship. The songs are very refined and of the highest class, rather Schumann-like in style, although altogether
original. Several artists have already prepared to use them in
concert, and they will no doubt meet with merited success, as
the elements of a successful song are all present in them. Tex-
ans are watching this young composer with great interest.'"

B35. "Radie Britain Returns From Texas." *Musical Courier* 95/12
(September 22, 1927): 22.

Announcement of Britain's return to Chicago and the opening of
her studio at the Girvin Institute.

B36. "Radie Britain Songs Win Dresden Praise." *Musical Courier* 95/16 (October 20, 1927): 38.

Brief translated quotations from German reviews of "Withered Flowers," "Open the Door to Me," and "Had I A Cave." *See:* W215c, W213b, and W210a.

B37. [Chicago, November 1927]

Review of *Nirvana,* performed at a recital of works by Texan composers on October 31st in San Antonio. "*Nirvana* is an art song that appeals to one's inner emotions, based on modern harmonies, but not astray from a melodic form, which gives the voice an opportunity to display a unique technic especially in pianissimo passages." *Nirvana* was awarded a first prize by Herbert Witherspoon, a voice teacher in Chicago, who plans to use it as part of his students' repertory. *See:* W218b.

B38. "Radie Britain's Composition Praised." *Musical Courier* 95/24 (December 15, 1927): 8.

Brief recapitulation of the *Amarillo Daily News*' report of the performance of *Nirvana* in San Antonio on October 31st. "Radie Britain . . . scored a tremendous success in San Antonio. Miss Britian has, largely through her own efforts, reached the enviable position which she now holds among composers, both here and abroad. She is recognized as one of the most brilliant young musical composers in this country." *See:* W218b.

B39. "Opera Composer Is Visitor Here." [Amarillo, December 1927?]

Short notice that Albert Noelte, "Miss Britain's teacher," was a guest of the Britains.

B40. "Tito Schipa." [December 1927]

Report of Schipa's recital in Chicago, December 15, 1927. "Among the English songs was one by Radie Britain, talented American composer(ess), now a resident of Chicago, which has been very well received, *Nirvana* ." *See:* W218c.

B41. "Tito Schipa at the Blackstone." *Musical Courier* 96/1 (January 5, 1928): 44.

Review of the operatic tenor's recital in Chicago. "A particularly catchy song was "Nirvana" by Radie Britain, gifted young American composer. The number, which was awarded first prize in a recent competition of Texas composers, is beautifully written, with melody effectively set in an individual harmonic scheme well scored for the voice, imaginative, original, and inspired." *See:* W218c.

B42. Hackett, Karleton. "Woman's Symphony Orchestra at the Goodman Theater." *Chicago Evening Post,* January 9, 1928.

"The symphony [sic] intermezzo of Radie Britain was played for the first time. It was pleasing, colorful music played with verve and the audience liked it. They called Miss Britain out a number of times." *See:* W2a.

B43. Stinson, Eugene. "With the Makers of Melody: Two Orchestras Heard." *Chicago Daily News,* January 9, 1928.

Brief review of *Symphonic Intermezzo* premiere in which "its beauty of color, its sensitiveness of orchestration and its musical freshness" are praised. *See:* W2a.

B44. "Schipa Sings Radie Britain's Prize Song, Nirvana." *Musical Courier* 96/2 (January 12, 1928): 35.

Review of Schipa's Chicago recital. Following the sudden death of her only sister, Britain visualized "the freed spirit of a beloved, departed one arrived at the sublime goal Nirvana, speeding from there its serene message of consolation." The "almost visionary" text of John Hall Weelock is combined with "a perfectly balanced melodic line" and a "soothing harmonic background . . . disclosing a startling variability in the selection and subtle combination of choice tone material." *See:* W218c.

B45. "Woman's Symphony Orchestra Adds to Sunday Music." *Musical Leader* 54/2 (January 12, 1928): 10.

The premiere of *Symphonic Intermezzo* "met with a most hearty reception, as well it deserved to, for in thematic material, in its development and in the rich scoring employed, the composer has proven that her creative talents have not only been well schooled but are of decidedly worth-while quality." *See:* W2a.

B46. Sanders, Troy. "The Woman's Symphony." [Chicago], January 13, 1928.

A brief review of the premiere of *Symphonic Intermezzo.* "The most unusual thing about the composition was its workmanship, showing as it did a well-balanced and full instrumentation, a good knowledge of the use of the orchestra as an instrument." *See:* W2a.

B47. "Woman's Symphony of Chicago Prospering Under Leginska." *Musical Courier* 96/2 (January 19, 1928): 48.

Discussion of Ethel Leginska's accomplishments includes a review of the premiere of *Symphonic Intermezzo*, "the work of a clever composer, who understands the orchestra and whose idiom is individual and inspired. It is well scored, and flows with melodies throughout that are original and beautiful. The composition was well liked, and the gifted composer had to bow many times in acknowledgement of most hearty applause." *See:* W2a.

B48. "The Woman's Symphony Orchestra of Chicago." *The Music News* (Chicago), [January 1928].

Review of the Chicago premiere of *Symphonic Intermezzo* . "Miss Britain . . . has already gained a fine reputation as theorist and composer. Her muse has been well trained in the old classic mold of composition, but often makes flights into the freer blue of 'modernism.' There is not in the work that continuous flow of melody which makes the usual quick appeal, but as full compensation there is a breadth and perfection of orchestration which is as wonderful as it is amazing. Rarely, indeed, has any short piece of orchestration been clothed in such voluminous harmony nor have many pieces moved along with such majesty of tread and completeness of full-tone effect. Miss Britain is, beyond doubt, full mistress of orchestration, and we may look confidently for many more and constantly improving works from her trenchant as well as graceful pen." *See:* W2a.

B49. M., N. "Amarillo Composer-Pianist Given Big Ovation in First Concert Here." *Amarillo Daily News*, February 11, 1928, 1-2.

Review of a recital in Amarillo by Radie Britain and tenor Arthur Kraft which included Miss Britain's performance of her Prelude and *Western Suite* for piano and, with Mr. Kraft, the songs "Had I A Cave" and "Nirvana." "That a composer, unlike a prophet is not without honor, and the greatest honor of all in his own country, was proved by the ovation with which Radie Britain was received last night at the auditorium at her first concert in her 'home town,' since she began to receive praise as one of the most talented of the younger generations of American composers." *See:* W82b, W83b, W210d, and W218d.

B50. Rackett, Alfred G. "Editor's Notebook: The Woman's Symphony." *The Intermezzo*, February 1928: 13.

Review of Chicago Woman's Symphony program includes the premiere of *Symphonic Intermezzo*. "It proved to be one of the oddest bits of fancy to which this scribe has ever harkened; is full of strange, uniquely placed chords and progressions, its quiet, almost apologetic opening succeeded by a majestic development that carries on all through the score until the sought for goal is found in the most majestic of climaxes. Scored in a fashion that commands respect and admiration, it is worthy of a place on any program. Here is talent unquestionable. Here is revealed a gift of no mean character for both composition and orchestration, with a concomitant flair of tone-coloring that is really surprising, if somewhat exotic in its nature. Regret was felt by those present that neither time, nor the ethics of the situation, gave opportunity for presentation of a further contribution from the same clever pen." *See:* W2a.

B51. "Radie Britain Winning Recognition from Press and Public." [February 1928]

Reporting the performance of several piano works and songs in a series of recitals held in Texas during February and the performance of *Symphonic Intermezzo* in Boston during the same month. "There are few American composers, especially among the women, who have won as much recognition from public and press alike as has Radie Britain recently."

B52. J., N. M. "Spotlight!" *Boston Transcript*, [February 1928].

Brief review of Boston performance of *Symphonic Intermezzo,* "conventional music of warm melodies, solidly orchestrated." *See:* W2b.

1930-1939

B53. "2 Illinois Composers Win Prizes During Contest at Hollywood." [July 21, 1930].

Notice that Radie Britain's symphonic poem *[Heroic Poem]* was awarded third prize in the Hollywood Bowl Prize Competition. "Foreign composers have figured largely in previous lists of winners. No prizes were awarded last year because entries failed to meet requirements. First prize winner this year was Arne Oldberg of Northwestern University, Evanston, Ill., for a piano concerto with orchestra. Second prize was won by Alois Reiser of Hollywood with a violoncello concerto with orchestra. . . ." *See:* W3.

B54. Moore, Edward. [Chicago, July 6, 1933].

Preview of upcoming concert. *Heroic Poem* , to be performed by the Chicago Philharmonic Orchestra, won first prize in a composition contest sponsored by the Hollywood Bowl. Britain describes the piece as "a series of moods. The first is that of a misty, dark morning, the morning of Lindbergh's flight. The rise of the plane submerges into Lindbergh's 'heroic theme' which is developed. Later there is a turmoil at sea, bringing in the motive of 'The Star Spangled Banner,' which is interpreted to mean that the American spirit must go on. There is a brief fughetta at the sight of Paris. A motive of 'Marseillaise' combines with 'The Star Spangled Banner' and the Lindbergh theme, and the plane descends in a mammoth climax." *See:* W3b.

B55. Barry, Edward. [Chicago, July 7, 1933].

Review of *Heroic Poem,* "a dramatic, well-knit and beautifully scored piece which is intended as a commemoration of Lindbergh's trans-Atlantic flight." *See:* W3b.

B56. Gunn, Glenn Dillard. "Philharmonic Orchestra of Chicago Makes Effective Debut in Concert at the Auditorium." *Chicago Herald and Examiner,* July 7, 1933, p. 15.

Review of "Radie Britain's *Heroic Poem,* a descriptive work commemorating Lindbergh's solo flight across the Atlantic. Miss Britain's composition is a well-made piece of its type, in which orchestral colors are skillfully used to suggest rather than to imitate. The sequence of moods, aptly defined, were doubtless good both as art and as psychology. I thought this music lacked conviction and characteristic melody, but nevertheless contrived to project its effects in persuasive fashion. It was cordially received and the composer was twice recalled to acknowledge the applause." *See:* W3b.

B57. Moore, Edward. "New Concert Series Given Warm Praise." *Chicago Daily Tribune,* July 7, 1933, p. 19.

Review of *Heroic Poem.* "The featured composition was Miss Britain's work on the Lindbergh flight. . . . She is a talented composer with a gift for melody and the further gift of being able to develop it in so interesting a manner that one's attention was easily diverted from the thought of a flight across the ocean to the music for its own sake. At its conclusion the composer was called to the stage and applauded with high enthusiasm." *See:* W3b.

B58. Stinson, Eugene. "Music Views." *Chicago Daily News*, July 7, 1933, p. 23.

> Review of *Heroic Poem.* "Miss Britain's short symphonic poem is cast in a derivative mold, but in this mold she works expertly and with sharply drawn and well-calculated effect. Her talent is well above the average and her future seems promising indeed." *See:* W3b.

B59. Devries, René. "Chicago Philharmonic Orchestra Makes Impression at First Concert." *Musical Courier* 107/4 (July 22, 1933): 9.

> Review of *Heroic Poem.* "Miss Britain . . . is a composer of high merit and her work met with distinct success. Though a young woman, she is not an ultra-modern composer inasmuch as she still believes in melody and refrains from writing cacaphonic music. . . . Miss Britain is a composer with imagination. Her pen is facile and her music closely woven. Her name was well associated with the other composers [Weber, Dvorak, and Liszt] on the same program." *See:* W3b.

B60. B., E. H. "Chicago Philharmonic Orchestra Proves an Organization of First Rank." *Music News* (Chicago), [July 1933].

> Review of *Heroic Poem.* "When the composition is regarded as pure music . . . it made a most agreeable impression, proving that its creator is possessed of a fine talent." *See:* W3b.

B61. Devries, Herman. "Chicago Philharmonic in Summer Debut." *The Chicago American*, [July 1933].

> Review of *Heroic Poem.* "The opening concert was a most auspicious one, having as its high point a novelty, the *Heroic Poem*, by the Chicago composer, Radie Britain. . . . Miss Britain has done a most brilliant piece of atmospheric writing. Without reference to any program notes . . . one can sense the mystery of the start in the darkness and fog, the drama of the heroic plunge into uncharted air, and the turmoil and furor and confusion of the descent at the flying field at Le Bourget . . . . We have heard other pieces of music inspired by Lindbergh's flight . . . but the palm goes to Miss Britain. . . . It was no novice hand that made use of the orchestra in this sure and practiced fashion. But the work is not simply a collection of startling descriptive effects . . . Miss Britain makes us feel the courage and the heroism that it took to make that pioneer flight all alone." *See:* W3b.

B62. "Amarillo Musician Receives Plaudits From Music Critics."
[Amarillo, July 1933.]

Report on the Chicago Philharmonic Symphony performance of
Heroic Poem, quoting the review from *The Chicago American*
excerpted above (*See:* B61). "Radie Britain Moeller, who is home
from Chicago for an extended visit . . . and who will give a com-
plimentary 30-minute organ concert tonight . . . at Polk Street
Methodist Church, has received the plaudits of some of the most
exacting music critics of the country." *See:* W3b.

B63. "Radie Britain's *Heroic Poem* Wins Acclaim of Chicago Music Critics." [Amarillo, July 1933.]

Summary of Chicago reviews for performance of *Heroic Poem* by
Chicago Philharmonic. "Mrs. Radie Britain Moeller is remembered here, by all who knew her, for her charming personality,
lovable disposition, high ideals of character and the musical
ability which, in her earlier years, gave promise of the fruition to
which it has now attained in such rich measure." *See:* W3b.

B64. "Chicago Symphonic Choir Honors Amarillo Composer." [Amarillo],
April 14, 1935.

Report on Chicago performance of *Drums of Africa*, with quotations from Chicago critics and the composer's description of the
music. "Judging by the reception—for it had to be repeated by
acclamation—the song will be popular before long" (Herman
Devries, critic). "'Drums of Africa' is built upon a primitive
rhythm played upon an African drum, forming a pedal point
throughout the composition" (Radie Britain). *See:* W161a.

B65. "Amarillo Composer Is Accepted For MacDowell Colony." Amarillo,
May 27, 1935.

Description of the MacDowell Colony with a notice of Miss Britain's acceptance to it for a period from June 20 to July 31.

B66. Thomas, Jessie M. "Women Composers Hold Conference At
Chautauqua." *Musical America* 55/13 (August 1935): 34.

Report on conference of American women composers at the
Chautauqua Summer Festival in July 1935, including note of
performance of *Prayer* by Miss Britain. *See:* W163a.

B67. "Local Woman's Music is Played At White House." Amarillo, April
17, 1936.

> "Mrs. Radie Britain Moeller, of Amarillo and Chicago, . . . was
> honored today when her compositions were played at the White
> House reception for [National] League [of American Penwomen]
> members. Mrs. Moeller, who attended the reception given by
> Mrs. Franklin D. Roosevelt, earlier in the week was awarded the
> prize for the best composition in a nation-wide competition. She
> has gained national recognition for her musical work." *See:*
> W43, W43b.

B68. "Program of Radie Britain's Compositions." *Musical Courier* 115/5
(January 30, 1937): 23.

> Brief notice that a program devoted entirely to original composi-
> tions by Radie Britain was given by the MacDowell Club of
> Amarillo, Texas, on January 18th.

B69. "MacDowell Music Club Will Present Program Thursday." Amarillo,
[January 1937].

> Announcement of a program of Miss Britain's compositions,
> including works for violin, voice, and piano, to be sponsored by
> the local music club.

B70. Barry, Edward. "Business Men's Orchestra Gives Varied Concert."
Chicago Daily Tribune, February 1, 1937, p. 17.

> Review of the premiere of the Overture to "Pygmalion" [later re-
> titled *Prelude to a Drama*]. "The Illinois Symphony Orches-
> tra . . . under Albert Goldberg's direction, gave a first perform-
> ance of the 'Pygmalion' Overture of Radie Britain, Chicago com-
> poser. Based on the legend of the sculptor who fell madly in love
> with the ivory maiden whose beauty his own chisel had fash-
> ioned, the overture does not on first hearing reveal its connec-
> tion with the tale. It does reveal itself as good music, fertile of
> idea, and opulently orchestrated." See: W1a.

B71. Gunn, Glenn Dillard. "Amy Neill 'Heroic' in Violin Concerto, Over-
> ture 'Pygmalion' Gets Fine Reading." *Chicago Herald and Exam-
> iner,* February 1, 1937, p. 15.

> Review of the premiere of the Overture to "Pygmalion" [later re-
> titled *Prelude to a Drama*]. ". . . Radie Britain, another gifted
> Chicagoan, heard her overture, 'Pygmalion,' played for the first
> time, as by the Illinois Symphony Orchestra, under that careful
> and competent conductor, Albert Goldberg, in the Great North-
> ern Theater. It is a fine work, well scored, cast in the authentic

idiom of the orchestra, modern, but making no effort at sensational dissonance. It has a brave set of melodies spontaneous in feeling and of genuine depth and beauty. The total impression was of music freely and eagerly made, entirely literate in its technical aspects, with plenty of imagination in its wealth of orchestral device, counter-melody and development." *See:* W1a.

B72. "Radie Britain's Overture Featured by Illinois Symphony." *Musical Courier* 115/7 (February 13, 1937), p. 10.

Review of the premiere of the Overture to "Pygmalion" [later retitled *Prelude to a Drama*]. "A modernist, Miss Britain nevertheless has written a melodious opus, superbly orchestrated, constructed on solid lines, original in concept . . . . the brief work met with the instant approval of the auditors, who recalled the composer several times." *See:* W1a.

B73. Devries, Herman. "Music in Review." *The Chicago American*, [February 1937].

Review of the premiere of the Overture to "Pygmalion" [later retitled *Prelude to a Drama*]. "Miss Britain has cleverly defined the love of the sculptor for his beautiful statue with flowing melodic lines, superb yet simple orchestration which marks it another success among her already long list." *See:* W1a.

B74. "Today's Radio Features." [March-April 1937.]

Brief notice of a broadcast of the *Infant Suite* "played by Alfred Wallenstein's orchestra on the 'Sinfonietta' program over Mutual from New York." *See:* W6b or 6c.

B75. "Radie Britain's Suite Heard." *Musical Courier* 118/2 (January 15, 1938): 24.

Brief review of the *Infant Suite* and the Philharmonic Woman's Symphony program of December 18, 1937. Miss Britain's *Suite* "proved to be the highlight of an interesting program." *See:* W6d.

B76. E., M. "Illinois Symphony Orchestra." *Music News* (Chicago), February 17, 1938, p. 4.

Brief review of the *Infant Suite* by "resident composer" Radie Britain in "its first [sic] Chicago performance" [in reality, the second Chicago performance]. "Here is an unusually interesting and well-constructed piece of work showing imagination and a definite style." *See:* W6e.

B77. Barry, Edward. "Concertgoers Like Piece by New Composer." *Chicago Daily Tribune*, [April 15, 1938].

Review of Maundy Thursday and Good Friday performances by the Chicago Symphony Orchestra. *Prelude to a Drama* "is an intense, highly mystical tone poem notable for the simplicity and directness of its material and for the great technical skill which it displays." *See:* W1b.

B78. Cassidy, Claudia. "On the Aisle: Frederick Stock and Chicago Symphony Orchestra Play Holy Week Music at Orchestra Hall." [*Chicago Journal of Commerce*, April 15, 1938].

Review of *Prelude to a Drama*. Described as "pure melody, opulently orchestrated, highly popular," *Prelude to a Drama* "might be any drama with jubilation as its goal, but which happens to derive from Schiller's 'Resurrection'." *See:* W1b.

B79. Devries, Herman. *The Chicago American* , [April 15, 1938].

Review of *Prelude to a Drama*. It "voices the divine in music form, and under Frederick Stock's baton the work made an even deeper impression than upon the first hearing when it was premiered with the Illinois Symphony under the direction of Albert Goldberg. Few women composers have been honored by our leading orchestras, and Stock and the Orchestral Association have done wisely in bringing to the public's notice a work of such great merit as to deserve a place in the regular repertory. Recalled several times at the conclusion of the work, Miss Britain can be sure of her success with audience, orchestra and director." *See:* W1b.

B80. Gunn, Janet. "Stock Salutes Good Friday." *Chicago Herald and Examiner*, April 15, 1938, p. 22.

Review of *Prelude to a Drama*. "There was a forecast of Easter in the *Prelude to a Drama* ." Miss Britain, "a native composer of fine imagination and growing resource, . . . was inspired to write this work by Schiller's poem, 'Resurrection'." *See:* W1b.

B81. Stinson, Eugene. "Music Views: Good Friday." *Chicago Daily News*, April 15, 1938, p. 14.

Review of the Maundy Thursday and Good Friday performances of *Prelude to a Drama*. The work "is not complex nor particularly weighty, but it is arrestingly rich in its orchestration and it moves of its own accord, importunately, rapidly and excitingly." *See:* W1b.

B82. "Stock Leads." [April 15, 1938].

Brief review of Holy Week performance of *Prelude to a Drama* "The coloring is adept and ingenious, but what is particularly striking about this work is its bold melodiousness and the spontaneity with which it moves from idea to idea." *See:* W1b.

B83. Barry, Edward. *Chicago Daily Tribune*, [April 25, 1938].

Brief review of premiere performance of *Rhapsodic Phantasie.* "The piece has the familiar Britain fluency of idea and richness of instrumentation." *See:* W4a.

B84. Cassidy, Claudia. "On the Aisle: Busy Sunday Brings Jascha Heifetz, a New *Carmen* and a Batch of Varied Concerts." [*Chicago Journal of Commerce*, April 25, 1938].

Review of the *Rhapsodic Phantasie.* It "shares the flow and sparkle that characterizes most of her work, being a rapturously scored rhapsody in the romantic mood with an eye over its shoulder on the Gershwin idiom." [Note: Miss Britain found the reference to Gershwin unjustified and took the critic to task over it.] *See:* W4a.

B85. Devries, René. "Chicago Symphony Orchestra Final Concerts Impressive." *Musical Courier* 117/9 (May 1, 1938): 38.

Review of *Prelude to a Drama.* "From the pen of the prolific American composer, Radie Britain, [the Prelude] premiered by the Illinois Symphony Orchestra a year ago, impressed even more favorably at these concerts. With scholarly orchestration and construction on solid lines, the overture contains melodious strains of beauty and poetic charm in its modern thematic idiom. The composition met with instantaneous success, its composer being recalled many times." *See:* W1b.

B86. Devries, René. "Choral, Orchestral and Solo Offering Delight Chicago." *Musical Courier* 117/10 (May 15, 1938): 26.

Review of *Rhapsodic Phantasie.* "Miss Britain does not favor the soloist but uses the piano solely as an integral part in her well orchestrated fantasie. Thus the fusion of piano and orchestral tone affords the soloist no display, requiring solely technical efficiency, which was fully met by Rose Goldberg." *See:* W4a.

B87. Devries, René. "Woman's Symphony Orchestra." *Musical Courier* 118/12 (December 15, 1938): 26.

> Review of *Light* on a program that included works by Bach and Borodin. "Miss Britain's new output indicates constant growth in this young American, whose always interesting idiom is further enhanced in atmospheric and descriptive pieces, for she visualizes the trend of modern times with inspired writing, clever in language and up to date in construction." *See:* W7a.

B88. Rackett, Alfred G. "Editor's Note Book: With Gladys Welge Conducting." *The Intermezzo*, January 1939, p. 8.

> Review of *Light*. "Radie Britain's brief tone-picture, *Light*, enjoying its Chicago premiere, lived up to the excellent reputation for original thought and enterprise which this clever composer has established. It is rather odd and peculiar in its construction and development; there is nothing familiar or hackneyed in outlines or traditions; dramatic and virile in its incisively-vivid patterns, and full of that verve and snap so vainly sought-after by most writers, the work progresses toward the ultimate of modern dynamics in a well-sustained routine of coordinated expressions which are apt to the subject portrayed. Edison would have hugely enjoyed this stirring, illuminating tribute to his scientific discoveries which Miss Britain has so deftly constructed. Truly, America is the land of future musical development." *See:* W7a.

B89. "For Release in Afternoon Newspapers." Federal Music Project, Works Progress Administration, February 4, 1939 (National Archives, Federal Music Project Files, Box 31).

> Press release concerning the performance of four songs with orchestral accompaniment ("In Living Ecstasy," "Sunken City," "Twilight Moon," and "Open the Door to Me"). "Radie Britain, who as a child in West Texas 'day-dreamed as I herded cattle on my snow-white cow pony,' that some day she must continue the study of composition in Europe, will hear in Chicago tomorrow (February 5) a world premiere performance of a new song cycle [sic] just completed by her. It will be performed by the WPA Illinois Symphony Orchestra, with a distinguished concert soprano, Esther Hart, as the soloist, and with Hans Levy Henoit at the desk as guest conductor. Since those days on the broad, wind-blown prairies, Miss Britain has achieved a considerable distinction as a composer. She did get to Europe, as she had dreamed, and made her debut as a composer in Munich in 1925, while she was a pupil of Dr. Albert Noelte. This was a seven-league stride for a spindle-legged little girl from the ranch who began her music studies at the age of seven at Clarendon

College, and who was graduated with highest honors. Other compositions by this Texas musician include a symphony and a symphonic intermezzo, a ballet, several choral works including an oratorio, and incidental music for the stage and motion pictures. Mrs. Florence Kerr, Assistant WPA Administrator for the Women's and Professional Division, and Dr. Nikolai Sokoloff, National Director of the Federal Music Project, both are admirers of Miss Britain's compositions. . . . Miss Britain now resides in Chicago." *See:* W225a, W226a, W228a, and W229a.

B90. Devries, René. "Chicago Music Fare Ranges from Russian Chorus to Berg Concerto." *Musical Courier* 109/5 (March 1, 1939): 18.

Review of songs with orchestral accompaniment. "Mr. Henoit shone also in Radie Britain's Four Songs—The Sunken City, Open the Door to Me, Twilight Moon and In Living Ecstasy, receiving first performances with orchestra. The first three, performed previously with piano accompaniment, gain considerably in musical value in their new garb because Miss Britain's modernistic orchestration emphasizes to a marked degree rather than alters the melodic line. Well sung by Esther Hart, soprano, the novelties made a decided impression." *See:* W225a, W226a, W228a, and W229a.

1940-1949

B91. Devries, Herman. "Music in Review." *The Chicago American,* [March 5, 1940].

Review of the Illinois Symphony Orchestra performance of *Southern Symphony.* "In Radie Britain's *Southern Symphony* Izler Solomon picked a winner. The piece is generously dotted with southern melodies, orchestrated in a manner that enhances tenfold the value of their simplicity in an instrumentation alive and palpitating with the ardor of Miss Britain's Texas ancestry." *See:* W9a.

B92. Devries, René. "Illinois Symphony Does Britain Symphony." *Musical Courier* 121/7 (April 1, 1940): 56.

Review of *Southern Symphony.* "Radie Britain is coming to the fore as one of the most representative American composers. Her latest output, *Southern Symphony,* . . . made a palpable hit. An ultramodernist in her musical idiom, Miss Britain nevertheless writes inspiringly and melodiously. Her orchestration might be bizarre but her ideas are sanely expressed and the symphony bears every earmark of an ingenious original composer." *See:* W9a.

B93. [Chicago, November 1940?].

> Review of String Quartet (1934). "Miss Britain's string quartet is
> a fine work with vital themes, an original approach to the form
> and string idiom, with lots of color and more sentiment than is
> customary among the moderns. The work won first prize offered
> by the American National Pen Women." *See:* W64, W46a.

B94. "Radie Britain Wins Composer's Prize." *New York Times*, March 28,
1941, p. 27.

> Notice that *Light* has been "declared the winner of the Boston
> Women's Symphony Society's national prize competition for
> women composers." A performance in Boston on May 25, 1941
> is announced. *See:* W7, 7b.

B95. Moody, Sally Brown. *San Diego Union*, [July 1941].

> Review of *Prison*. "A first performance of *Prison* by the San
> Diego Symphony, a short, symbolic work scored for small or-
> chestra by the noted composer, Radie Britain, was most inter-
> esting and peculiarly poignant and nostalgic in content." *See:*
> W15d.

B96. "Studio Composer is Awarded National Prize." San Diego, [1941].

> Notice that "Radie Britain, composer and pianist, who has re-
> cently opened a studio in Coronado, has just been notified that
> she has been awarded the national prize among American
> women composers for her piece for string orchestra which will
> be presented in Los Angeles in August. [*See:* Suite for Strings,
> W16.] The National Musical Society S. A. I. sponsored the con-
> test. Miss Britain has been engaged for master classes in the
> Hollywood Professional School, also for the Southern California
> Institute of Music in San Diego. Coronadans, who are musically
> inclined and have children who need special training, will be
> delighted to know that they have the opportunity of attending
> classes taught by one who has gained a national reputation for
> efficiency in music and composition. She will accept a limited
> number of pupils for class and private lessons."

B97. Jones, Isabel Morse. "Russian Pianist Featured at Embassy
Auditorium." *Los Angeles Times*, January 22, 1942, part 2, p.
19.

> Review of *Prelude to a Drama*. "Miss Britain was present to
> acknowledge the applause. Her short orchestral work is roman-
> tic writing. The orchestration is rich and has more in it to re-
> mind one of Franck and Wagner than Harris or Copland. Her

works have been played here before and this one was performed in Chicago several times. It is built on simple themes and exhibits wide knowledge of instrumentation. She has a long list of orchestral, choral and chamber works to her credit." *See:* W1e.

B98. Rogers, John M. "Music Review." *Daily News* (Los Angeles), January 22, 1942, p. 22.

> Review of *Prelude to a Drama.* "This was the first performance in California of the prelude, which was suggested by Schiller's poem, 'Resurrection.' It may be best described as 'American Modern,' but happily there are [no] xylophone or flute solos or staccato cymbals suggestive of scurrying feet, subways or other big city noises. I talked with Miss Britain after the performance and learned that her 'String Quartet' had been performed for the First Lady at the White House and would be played in Los Angeles next month." *See:* W1e, W46b.

B99. Saunders, Richard D. "Pianist Wins Ovation At Embassy Concert." *Hollywood Citizen-News,* January 22, 1942.

> Review of *Prelude to a Drama.* "It proved an emotionally warm work, its melodic themes deftly developed in a conservative yet individual manner, its orchestration made with sensitivity in instrumental colorings." *See:* W1e.

B100. Cage, John. "Chavez and the Chicago Drouth." *Modern Music* 19/3 (March-April, 1942): 185-86. Quoted in *John Cage,* ed. Richard Kostelanetz (New York: Praeger, 1970), pp. 62-64.

> A review, favoring Chávez at the expense of Miss Britain and Cadman, of the Illinois WPA Symphony premiere of Miss Britain's *Drouth* and performances by the Chicago Symphony Orchestra with visiting composer Carlos Chávez conducting three of his own works, Nicloai Berezowsky's Concerto for viola and orchestra, and Cadman's *Pennsylvania Symphony* . "The Illinois WPA Symphony, which is to be commended for its many first performances of contemporary works, gave on this occasion two very dull *premières:* Radie Britain's *Drouth* and Leos Jánacek's *Lachian Dances. . . .* Miss Britain's *Drouth,* like Cadman's *Symphony,* also needed an illustrative film, particularly for the plaintive cowboy song, which is heard toward the end of the composition, 'expressing his loneliness and desolation as he sees the land blown away.' The strings did most of the blowing and sighing. At one point a ratchet electrified the wind section and for a moment there were interesting jagged sounds. But these were written for a decorative-dramatic effect and not as an organic part of the composition. They were followed by moaning muted violins. Miss Britain is said, through this work,

to exhibit her kinship with the great Middle West. . . . Miss Britain and Mr. Cadman have accepted certain literary and intellectual concepts of the American scene, which they have illustrated musically. The music is recognizably regional according to one's knowledge of the conditions that prompted it; it is not an expression in musical terms of a close contact with the country." *See:* W11a.

B101. "New Symphony By Local Composer To Make Debut." *Amarillo News-Globe,* January 9, 1944.

Notice of performance and biographical sketch. "The tone poem *San Luis Rey* . . . opens with bells of the mission followed by the theme of the Franciscan monks as they walk slowly through the mission in silent meditation. The church choir is heard in the distance, and the ancient fountain is depicted by a flute solo in quicker tempo. A return to the first theme brings the composition to a close, with a faint coloring of bells and their overtones." *See:* W18a.

B102. T., B. B. "Artists Given Acclaim in Concert Here." *Amarillo Daily News,* February 6, 1946, p. 10.

Review of *Prison.* "The Municipal Auditorium was near-capacity last night when Amarillo's music-minded turned out to welcome with genuine appreciation two of its daughters presented in the Philharmonic Symphony Orchestra concert. Radie Britain's composition, ultramodern in scope, was received enthusiastically. . . . [The other "daughter" was a pianist who played the Liszt E-flat Concerto.] Miss Britain's Lament, 'Prison,' is a portrait based on the constant rhythm of drums and bass viol, forming a background of monotony for the plaintive melody. It was beautiful in its quiet weirdness." *See:* W15e.

B103. "Southland Composers' Music To Be Featured." *Glendale News-Press,* April 3, 1947, section B, p. 1.

Preview of *San Luis Rey.* "Radie Britain is one of the few American women composers of symphonic music who has received wide recognition. Many of her compositions have been performed and she was the first woman to win the coveted Juilliard Foundation prize for orchestral works. This particular work, 'Heroic Poem,' was performed in Hollywood Bowl in 1930. Daughter of a Texas rancher, she had to break down her father's opposition to European study before she went to Munich after attending the American Conservatory of Music in Chicago. The composer and her sculptor husband, Edgardo Simone, with their [sic] young daughter, reside in the Hollywood hills, pursuing their artistic careers together. The Britain composition chosen for local performance Monday night is 'San Luis Rey' from 'Franciscan Sketches,' a short, light work." *See:* W18c.

B104. Reeder, Beckie. "'All Amarillo' Concert Given Top Reception By Audience." *Amarillo Daily News,* April 9, 1947, p. 12.

Review of *Serenata Sorrentina.* "Mrs. Simone, a native of Amarillo, composes in the modern idioms. The 'Serenata Sorrentina' was noteworthy for its unusual melodic line and orchestra coloring. Mr. Barron and the orchestra portrayed well its essential style and intonation." *See:* W23a.

B105. Reis, Claire. *Composers in America.* 1947; reprint New York: Da Capo, 1977.

Biographical information and list of works for composers of the 1940s who had written chamber or orchestral music and who had received at least one major performance. Along with Miss Britain, the volume includes woman composers Marion Bauer, Amy Beach, Jeanne Behrend, Evelyn Breckman, Gena Branscombe, Ulric Cole, Ruth Crawford, Mabel Wheeler Daniels, Vivian Fine, Florence G. Galajikian, Miriam Gideon, Mary Howe, Dorothy James, Beatrice Laufer, Eda Rapoport, Louise Talma, and Mabel Wood-Hill.

B106. "Symphony to repeat 'Nocturne' [sic]." *Atlanta Constitution,* April 4, 1948, p. 7-B.

Review of *Nocturn* and notice of future performance. "Radie Britain's *Nocturne* will be given a repeat performance by the Altanta Symphony Orchestra in a special concert Wednesday. . . . The brilliant orchestral score was given its Atlanta premiere last Sunday as part of the Orchestra's regular subscription concert. It was warmly received by the large audience. A meditative score, *Nocturne* reflects the serenity of the night. It is a true tone picture. With each of its many subdued and beautifully phrased passages, the listener constantly is aware of the scene it describes. . . . Henry Sopkin will conduct." *See:* W5c.

B107. Jones, Howell. "Emory Throng Acclaims Atlanta Symphony Show." *Atlanta Constitution,* April 8, 1948, p. 7.

Review of *Nocturn.* "One of the highlights of the program was Radie Britain's *Nocturne* [sic]. A tone picture, Miss Britain's work was given an excellent reading by Sopkin and the orchestra. All of the orchestra's 1,000 listeners were charmed by the excellent construction and poetic content of the score which pictured perfectly night and all its mystery." *See:* W5d.

B108. "Famous Composer Visits Here, Amarillo's Own Radie Britain."
The Amarillo Times, July 12, 1949.

Notice of Miss Britain's visit to her parents' home, list of recent
and upcoming performances, and a brief biographical sketch.
"Radie Britain's recipe [sic] for a composer is 'to have fantasy, a
sensitive ear and great technical ability. Absolute pitch is not
necessary, but a good relative pitch is needed.' From her girl-
hood surroundings as a rancher's daughter, she gets the inspiration for much of her music. Two of her most successful compositions with the atmosphere of the West are *Red Clay* and
"Lasso of Time." Because of this, she has been dubbed the
'Cowgirl Composer'." *See:* W22 and W231.

1950-1957

B109. Stevens, Halsey. "Program Notes: *Prelude to a Drama.*" *Los
Angeles Philharmonic Symphony Magazine* (February 16-17,
1950): 457.

Brief explanation of the Greek myth of Pygmalion and Galatea
that inspired the Prelude. The author makes no mention of
Miss Britain's training, experience, or musical style. Pieces by
Ernest Bloch, Dvorak, Ernst Toch, and Elgar on the same program receive fuller treatment. *See:* W1g.

B110. Goldberg, Albert. "The Sounding Board: Well-Balanced Music
Event Features Cellist." *Los Angeles Times*, February 17, 1950,
p. 23.

Review of *Prelude to a Drama.* "Radie Britain is one of the few
contemporary women composers to attempt the larger forms,
and her 'Prelude to a Drama' emerged as a fluent piece of writing, well orchestrated in a fulsome Straussian manner with a
passionate flow of melody to illustrate its inspiration from the
classic Pygmalion legend." *See:* W1g.

B111. Greene, Patterson. "Philharmonic Music Likable." *Los Angeles
Examiner*, February 17, 1950, p. 25.

Review of *Prelude to a Drama.* "Opening the concert was Texas-
born Radie Britain's "Prelude to a Drama," in which workaday
but workable material is suffused with agreeably lush orchestral
coloration. Miss Britain was present to bow to the applause,
which was warm." *See:* W1g.

B112. Kendall, Raymond. "Joseph Schuster Plays Dvořák Concerto With Philharmonic." *The Mirror* (Los Angeles), February 17, 1950, p. 37.

Review of *Prelude to a Drama.* "Miss Britain's "Prelude to a Drama" is a bustling program opener which gives the impression that it might wear a little thin on subsequent hearings." *See:* W1g.

B113. Goss, Madeline. *Modern Music Makers.* New York: E. P. Dutton, 1952.

A "life and works" article on Miss Britain in a volume which includes similar entries for "most of today's leading composers," although the subjects are limited to American-born composers whom the author was able to interview. Other composers represented in the volume are Antheil, Barber, Marion Bauer, Robert Russell Bennett, Bergsma, Leonard Bernstein, Blitzstein, Gena Branscombe, John Alden Carpenter, Copland, Cowell, Creston, Mable Daniels, Della Joio, Diamond, Foss, Gould, Gruenberg, Hanson, Harris, Mary Howe, Ives, Harl McDonald, Douglas Moore, Piston, Riegger, Bernard Rogers, Schuman, Sessions, Harold Shapiro, Sowerby, Still, Louise Talma, Deems Taylor, Virgil Thomson.

B114. T., B. B. "Full House Hears Symphony Concert." *Amarillo Daily News,* February 23, 1955, p. 17.

Review of *Nocturn* for small orchestra, "a pleasant blending of the old and the modern. It was received with high enthusiasm, an expression for both the orchestra and the work itself." *See:* W5g.

B115. Roller, A. Clyde. [Amarillo, February 1955].

Review of *Nocturn,* "music written in the modern idiom with themes that are easily understood, being orchestrated in an exceptional manner, showing a rare mastery of technique." *See:* W5g.

B116. "Radie Britain Receives Award." *Amarillo Sunday News-Globe,* May 15, 1955, p. 18-B.

Announcement of the first prize awarded to *Barcarola,* for violin and piano, in a statewide competition in California. (*See:* W54.) One of Britain's compositions was to be performed the following month by the United States Air Force Symphony in a Scandinavian tour. *See:* W1k-W1o.

B117. Dinan, Patsy. "European Music Critics Have Kind Words for Britain Work." *Amarillo Globe-Times*, [Fall 1955].

Translated quotations from European newspaper criticisms of *Prelude to a Drama* as performed by United States Air Force Orchestra on spring 1955 tour and reprint of Miss Britain's essay "Composer Looks at American Music." *See:* B1; *See:* W1k-W1o.

B118. "Britain." *Music of the West Magazine* 11 (May 1956): 11.

Notice that "Radie Britain's *Heroic Poem* for orchestra was performed March 11, by the Atlanta, Georgia, Symphony Orchestra on their Spring Music Festival, with Henry Sopkin conducting. This composition was awarded the Juilliard publication award. Miss Britain is the first woman to receive this distinguished honor. *Heroic Poem* was awarded the third prize in an international contest sponsored by the Hollywood Bowl." *See:* W3, 3g.

B119. McReynolds, Bill. "Honors at Symphony Shared By Composer and Conductor." *Amarillo Globe-Times*, October 24, 1956, p. 37.

Review of the premiere of *Cowboy Rhapsody*. "Miss Britain's latest work, *Cowboy Rhapsody*, was premiered before the current season's largest audience. To her work, Miss Britain inserted a gloss of feminine understanding in capturing the vastness of the Western plains, the lonely life of the cowboy and a feeling of the prevalent ruggedness. She has done this in a symphonic movement without sacrificing the techniques that are essential to this type of music. . . . In toto, the magnitude of Western space and life was sounded." *See:* W30a.

B120. McReynolds, Bill. "Premier of Hometowner's Work Pleases." *Amarillo Daily News*, October 24, 1956, p. 17.

Review of the premiere of *Cowboy Rhapsody*. "The wide-open space of the range and its settlement was sounded last night, when the Amarillo Symphony premiered Radie Britain's *Cowboy Rhapsody*. The Amarillo composer was honored by a stage appearance before intermission. Her parents . . . also attended. . . . Mr. Britain is a member of the Western Cowpunchers Association. The Cowpunchers, who were guests of the Symphony, sat in a special section. They also heard Miss Britain's *Rhapsody*, dedicated to the pioneers—such as themselves—of West Texas. In her composition, Miss Britain softened memory of rugged pioneer settlement with feminine understanding. By use of Indian ritual-type themes, she conveyed a sense of resistance. Then the beat quickened with a well-developed clarinet solo to introduce the cowboy, his lonely life, and final conquest." *See:* W30a.

B121. "Britain," *Music of the West Magazine* 11 (December 1956): 11.

Notice of the October 23 premiere of *Cowboy Rhapsody* in Amarillo, with an excerpt from Amarillo's *News-Globe* newspaper. "*Cowboy Rhapsody* has been a dream in Miss Britain's mind for many years. It was a challenge to try to put cowboy tunes into counterpoint treatment and not lose the spirit of the West. The music is in three sections, but of one movement. It depicts the vastness and the nobility of the plains—the lonesome cowboy's lament. And the finale is filled with galloping tunes. Beside Miss Britain were her loving and guiding parents. . . . Together with the audience, they listened to the Cowboy Rhapsody dedicated to the pioneers of West Texas." *See:* W30a.

B122. "Texas Orchestra Offers Premiere of Texas Work." *Music Clubs Magazine* 36/3 (January 1957): 36.

Notice of the premiere of *Cowboy Rhapsody. See:* W30a.

B123. "Britain." *Music of the West Magazine,* 12 (May 1957), p. 7.

Notice that "Radie Britain, American woman composer of Hollywood, California, has again received national recognition. On Feburary 19, 1957, the Pan American Union, in the Hall of the Americas, presented the first performance of her *Saturnale,* symphonic poem, with T/Sgt. William DuPree, tenor, as singer. The Concert of Music of the Americas, by members of the District of Columbia Chapter of the National Association for American Composers and Conductors and other American Composers with The United States Air Force Symphony Orchestra, conducted by Colonel George S. Howard, programmed works of Jose Marria Castro, Max Seeboth, Serge de Gastyne and Radie Britain. The tone poem *Saturnale* was inspired by the ancient Roman God, Saturn. His reign, called the Golden Age, was a reign marked by peace, happiness, and conten'ment. Legend tells us that the Feast of Saturn, annually celebrated in the middle of December, was the occasion for gay festivities. Miss Britain's *Saturnale* depicts the celebration of a festival in the spirit of that fabled Golden Age and bears the following general program notes: *Saturnale* is 'A wild Bacchanale—the opening by the singing of the fruit vendor—then slowly going into the dances of the fiesta with much wine, drinking, and celebration'." *See:* W14b.

B124. "Premiere Performances." *The Musical Courier* 155/7 (May 1957): 6.

Notice of February 19 premiere in Washington, D.C. and radio broadcast to South America of *Saturnale*. *See:* W14b.

B125. "Britain." *Music of the West Magazine* 12 (July 1957): 9.

Notice that "Radie Britain's orchestral composition *Heroic Poem* [sic] will be performed in Moscow, Russia, on an all-American program to be given by the Moscow Symphony Orchestra conducted by Konstantin Ivanov. He will also include compositions by Bloch and Gershwin. *Heroic Poem*, dedicated to Lindbergh's flight to Paris, was given its world premiere by Howard Hanson with the Rochester Symphony Orchestra. It has received many major performances including the Chicago Philharmonic, Chicago Woman's Symphony, Atlanta Symphony, Boston Woman's Symphony and the New York Philharmonic Society. . . . [*See:* W3; *Heroic Poem* was never performed in Moscow, but *Prelude to a Drama* was. *See:* W1t.] This past season her *Saturnale* received its world premiere by the U.S. Air Force Symphony, Colonel George Howard conducting. [*See:* W14b.] *Cowboy Rhapsody* received its first performance by the Amarillo Symphony, Clyde Roller conducting. [*See:* W30a.] Ricordi's of Sao Paulo, Brazil, is releasing the publication *Minha Terra*, arranged for two pianos." *See:* W143.

B126. "Premiere Performances." *The Musical Courier* 156/9 (July 1957): 6.

Notice of the premiere of *Cowboy Rhapsody*, "dedicated to the pioneers of West Texas," by the Amarillo Symphony. *See:* W30a.

B127. "News in Brief." *The Musical Courier* 156 (15 December 1957): 6.

Notice of award. "For her outstanding contribution in musical composition, the National League of American Pen Women has made an award of merit to the composer Radie Britain. The presentation was made in Washington October 12." The short article also notes that Dr. Leo Podolsky has included "Minha Terra" in his recommended repertoire, and that the work will soon be performed by ten pianists at the Amarillo Arts Conservatory. *See:* W143.

B128. Park, Sarah. "Composer Has Firm Ideas On Music, Creative Arts." [Honolulu, Hawaii, 1957?].

Brief biographical sketch and discussion of the music of Radie Britain, who is in Hawaii to find inspiration for a new work.

1960-67

B129. "Opera By Radie Britain To Have World Premiere." *Music of the West Magazine* 16 (June 1961): 13.

Notice of the premiere of *Kuthara* planned for June 24 in Santa Barbara, California, "under the auspices of the Santa Barbara chapter of the National Society of Arts and Letters. The libretto is the work of Lester Luther, voice coach of Paramount Studios. Artistic direction is in the hands of Margaret Stromer. . . . *Kuthara* is modern, in three acts. . . ." *See:* W157a.

B130. "The Composer." *Musical Courier* 163/9 (August 1961): 39.

Brief announcement of the premiere of the opera *Kuthara (The Scythe)* in Santa Barbara on June 24. *See:* W157a.

B131. Everett, Alta Turk. "New Opera Premiered in Outdoor Setting." *Music of the West Magazine* 16 (August 1961): 6.

Review of premiere of *Kuthara,* "presented June 24 in the beautiful gardens at the home of Mr. and Mrs. James G. McNary. The performance was sponsored by the Santa Barbara chapter of the National Society of Arts and Letters as its first scholarship fund benefit to assist young artists. . . . The setting was most appropriate for the dramatic and tragic tale by Lester Luther, of an overpowering mother's love for a son on a small farm in the New England Hills. . . . The well-chosen cast gave a realistic portrayal of the new and demanding music. . . . Radie Britain at the piano provided a masterful accompaniment." *See:* W157a.

B132. Sanders, A. W. *Hollywood Citizen News,* [October 1961].

Review of *Saint Francis of Assisi.* "World premiere of Radie Britain's *Saint Francis of Assisi* brought to light a beautifully orchestrated, appealingly melodic work that retains the romantic feeling while employing modern tone coloring with commendable restraint and consistent skill. It was free in form, treating its thematic material in a rather declamatory fashion appropriate to the title." *See:* W17a.

B133. Bivins, Sally. "Music of the Plains Inspires Artist." *Amarillo Sunday News-Globe*, September 2, 1962.

> Summary of Miss Britain's recent performances and pending compositions, with her thoughts on the current state of American music and women in the arts. "America has so much talent she hardly knows what to do with it all, Miss Britain believes. . . . Miss Britain feels no despair about the current state of American popular music. She is even tolerant toward teenage musical fads. 'After all, they are for a special purpose—dancing. That requires beat and excitement and drive. It is bad only when that is the sole form of music a person listens to or can enjoy. . . . More and more women are becoming fine artists. . . . It simply means that we must work twice as hard to succeed in the arts, but we can do it if we are willing to dedicate ourselves'."

B134. Collier, Virginia Rollwage. "Our Most Honored Artist-Composer." *The Pen Woman* (April 1963).

> Biographical article. "Radie Britain, Los Angeles Branch, has written more orchestral compositions and received more international acclaim and awards (more than fifty) than any other woman composer. She composes with great power of emotion scenes in which she becomes deeply involved and re-creates the excitement of contemporary situations. Believing in inspiration and activism, she says of her work: 'I feel that music is written through me, rather than by me'."

B135. Howard, John Tasker. *Our American Music: A Comprehensive History from 1620 to the Present.* Fourth edition. New York: Thomas Y. Crowell, 1965, p. 521.

> Short paragraph with major biographical information and important works.

B136. Cunningham, Carl. "Houston Symphony Plays New Music at University." *Houston Post*, April 19, 1967, sect. 4, p. 6.

> Brief review of *Cosmic Mist Symphony*. "The Houston Symphony began its eight-day Symposium of New Music at the University of Houston's Cullen Auditorium. Tuesday's opening event was a reading rehearsal of 18 new orchestral works. . . . [including] a long and overblown *Cosmic Mist Symphony* by Radie Britain, a programmatic work that gave the orchestra some technical problems in its final movement." *See:* W33a.

B137. Holmes, Ann. "U H Symposium of New Music Has Strange, Welcome Sounds." *Houston Chronicle*, April 19, 1967, p. 18.

Brief review of *Cosmic Mist Symphony.* "The University of Houston's first Symposium of New Music is underway at Cullen Auditorium. . . . Composers from many parts of the country are here and others are expected. . . . Among the composers are five from Houston and one lady composer from Greenville, S.C., Jean Eichelberger Ivey. . . . Composers from as far away as Paris and Rome are represented. . . . In *Cosmic Mist* Symphony, Radie Britain of Hollywood explores the weird voids of cold Earth before man and moves on, through nebulous time, to Nuclear Fission. His [sic] description calls for a musical detonation, and 'exciting rhythm of the bombardment of the atom'." *See:* W33a.

1970-1981

B138. Hale, Richard. "Brentwood-Westwood Symphony Presents Impressive Program." *Evening Outlook* (Santa Monica, California), March 11, 1971, p. 14.

Review of the "world premiere of 'The Builders,' a brief patriotic chorus by the well-known Los Angeles composer, Radie Britain. . . . Radie Britain's composition was inspired by a short poem written by her daughter, Lerae Britain, and her well-turned music enhanced the direct idealism of the words with orchestral fullness." *See:* W199a.

B139. "Women in Music." *Pan Pipes of Sigma Alpha Iota* 67/2 (January 1975): 2-7.

Report on concert and panel discussion on women in music held at California State University at Los Angeles in the summer of 1974. Includes biographical information on Miss Britain and eleven other women composers.

B140. Borroff, Edith. "The Fairbank Collection." *College Music Symposium* 16 (Spring 1976): 105-22.

Notes presence of songs by Miss Britain in the collection of soprano Janet Fairbank, assembled in the 1930s and 1940s, housed in the Newberry Library in Chicago.

B141. Morrow, Grace. "Texas Can Brag About Its Women Composers." *Reporter-News* (Abilene, Texas), March 25, 1977, p. B-3.

Brief discussion of the work of Miss Britain and eight other women composers born or presently active in Texas.

B142. *Catalogue of Contemporary American Women Composers.* West Babylon, New York: Harold Branch Publishing, Inc., 1977.

Catalogue of works by women composers published by Harold Branch, with biographical information on Miss Britain and twelve others.

B143. Finch, Shari. "'Escape . . . Conformity': Local Author Describes Creative Process." *Desert Community News,* May 31, 1978.

Promotion of the book *Composer's Corner,* with quotations and biographical background. *See:* B6.

B144. Finger, Mary. "There's always a song in her heart: Composer-author Radie Britain Achieves Self-fulfillment Through Music." *Palm Desert Post,* July 13, 1978, p. B-4.

Biographical article with discussion of works and creative process. Promotion of book *Composer's Corner.* "Radie Britain meditates and the music flows through her being. . . . The notes are there at her fingertips and come as fast as she can write them. . . . Radie enjoys all aspects of living but says her happiest moments are when she sees her performances are understood, and when she feels she has 'lighted a spark' in her students of harmony and composition." *See:* B6.

B145. LePage, Jane Weiner. *Women Composers, Conductors, and Musicians of the Twentieth Century: Selected Biographies.* Metuchen, New Jersey: Scarecrow Press, 1980.

A "life and works" article based on an interview with Miss Britain. "Britain's ability to create musical beauty in over one hundred and fifty classical compositions is enhanced by her power to eloquently communicate with the written word. Miss Britain writes that a person must 'escape the evils of conformity in order to create'."

B146. Cohen, Aaron I., ed. *International Encyclopedia of Women Composers.* New York: Bowker, 1981.

Biographical paragraph and list of selected works.

Appendix I:
Chronological List of Works

[WORKS COMPOSED IN THE SAME YEAR ARE LISTED IN ALPHABETICAL ORDER; ORIGINAL WORKS PRECEDE ARRANGEMENTS]

1925   *Had I A Cave*, W210
          Half Rising Moon, W211
          Ocean Moods, W81
          Prelude, W82
          Western Suite, W83

1926   *Immortality*, W212
          Open the Door to Me (solo voice and piano), W213
          Sunken City (solo voice and piano), W214
          Withered Flowers, W215

1927   *Berceuse*, W216
          Hail Texas, W217
          Portrait of Thomas Jefferson (Epic Poem), W43
          Nirvana, W218

1928   *Legend*, W44
          Prelude To A Drama, W1
          Symphonic Intermezzo, W2

1929   *Dance Grotesque* (solo piano), W84
          Dance Grotesque (violin and piano), W45
          Heroic Poem, W3
          Requiem, W219
          Shepherd in the Distance, W150

1933   *Rhapsodic Phantasie* (piano and orchestra), W4
          The Wanderer's Evening Song, W220
          Wheel of Life, W151

1934   *Drums of Africa* (SATB), W161
       Drums of Africa (TTBB), W162
       Nocturn, W5
       Prayer, W163
       String Quartet, W46
       When We Shall Part, W221

1935   *Dicky Donkey* (SATB), W164
       Dicky Donkey (SSAA), W165
       Fairy of Spring, W166
       Haunted, W167
       Infant Suite (solo piano), W85
       Infant Suite (small orchestra), W6
       Light, W7
       Noontide, W168
       Prison Lament) (violin and piano), W47
       Prison(Lament) (Russian instruments), W8
       Rain, W169
       Southern Symphony, W9

1936   *Baby I Can't Sleep* (chorus), W170
       Baby I Can't Sleep (solo voice), W222

1937   *Elegy,* W223
       Immortality (chorus), W171
       Ubiquity, W152

1938   *The Chateau* (solo piano), W86
       The Chateau (violin and piano), W48
       In Living Ecstasy (solo voice and piano), W224
       In Living Ecstasy (solo voice and orchestra), W225
       Little Spaniard, W87
       Sunken City (solo voice and orchestra), W226
       Twilight Moon (chorus), W172
       Twilight Moon (solo voice and piano), W227
       Twilight Moon (solo voice and orchestra), W228

1939   *Canyon* (orchestra), W10
       Canyon (piano sketch), W88
       Drouth (orchestra), W11
       Drouth (solo piano), W89
       Nature Ushers in the Dawn, W173
       Ontonagon Sketches, W12
       Open The Door To Me (solo voice and orchestra), W229
       Pastorale (orchestra), W13
       Pastorale (two pianos), W140
       Saturnale, W14

1940   *Chipmunks,* W49
        Dance Grotesque (two flutes), W50
        The Earth Does Not Wish for Beauty (chorus and piano), W174
        The Earth Does Not Wish for Beauty (solo voice), W230
        Geppetto's Toy Shop, W90
        I'se Comin' Lord To You, W175
        Lasso Of Time (chorus), W176
        Lasso Of Time (solo voice), W231
        Prison(Lament) (small orchestra), W15
        Serenada Del Coronado, W91
        Stillness (solo voice), W232
        Suite for Strings, W16

1941   *Humble Me,* W177
        Life's Ebb and Flow, W233
        Saint Francis of Assisi (orchestra), W17
        Saint Francis of Assisi (solo piano), W92
        San Luis Rey (orchestra), W18
        San Luis Rey (solo piano), W93
        Stillness (chorus), W178

1942   *Eternal Cycle,* W234
        Love Me Today, W235
        Phantasy (oboe and orchestra), W19
        Phantasy (oboe and piano), W51
        Phantasy (oboe, harp and piano), W52
        Serenade (solo voice), W236
        Silver Wings, W237
        We Believe, W20

1944   *Serenade* (violin and piano), W53

1945   *All Alone on the Prairie,* W238
        Dance of the Clown, W94
        Jewels of Lake Tahoe, W21
        More Rain, More Rest, W239

1946   *Happyland,* W153
        Red Clay (orchestra), W22
        Red Clay (solo piano), W95
        Serenata, Sorrentina (orchestra), W23
        Serenata, Sorrentina (solo piano), W96
        Umpqua Forest, W24

1947   *Love Song of the Taj Mahal,* W240
        Paint Horse and Saddle (orchestra), W25
        Paint Horse and Saddle (piano sketch), W97

1948   *Barcarola* (solo piano), W98
       Barcarola (violin and piano), W54
       The Chalice (solo voice), W241
       Goddess of Inspiration (solo piano), W99
       Goddess of Inspiration (solo voice), W242
       The Juggler, W100
       Vision of Loveliness, W243

1949   *Barcarola* (chorus), W179
       Enchantment, W101
       Escape, W102
       Farewell at Dawn, W244
       Heel and Toe, W103
       Torillo, W104
       Your Hand, W245

1950   *How to Play the Piano*, W105
       Intermezzo, W55
       Red Clay (ballet), W154
       Rhapsodic Phantasie (two pianos), W141

1951   *Angel Chimes* (solo piano), W106
       Angel Chimes (two pianos), W142
       The Chalice (chorus), W180
       Chicken in the Rough (orchestra), W26
       Chicken in the Rough (piano sketch), W107
       Little Man (solo voice), W246
       Wings of Silver, W108

1952   *Carillon*, W155
       Love Still Has Something of the Sea (solo voice), W247

1953   *Cactus Rhapsody* (orchestra), W27
       Cactus Rhapsody (solo piano), W109
       The Earth Does Not Wish for Beauty (chorus and orchestra), W181
       Joy, W110
       Reflections, W111
       Solar Joy (solo piano), W112
       The Spider and the Butterfly, W156

1954   *Angel Chimes* (orchestra), W28
       Mexican Weaver, W113

1955   *Adoration* (solo piano), W114
       Casa del Sogno (violin and piano), W56
       Soil Magic, W248
       Solar Joy (orchestra), W29

1956   *Cowboy Rhapsody*, W30
        Ensenada, W115
        Minha Terra (Barrozo Netto) (two pianos), W143
        Song of the Joshua, W116
        The Star and the Child (SATB), W182
        The Star and the Child (SSA), W183

1957   *Le Petit Concerto*, W144
        Venete, Felii Audite Me, W184

1958   *Barcarola* (eight celli and vocalise), W57
        Casa del Sogno (oboe and piano), W58
        Minha Terra (Barrozo Netto) (orchestra), W31
        Revelation, W249
        Sonata, Op. 17, W117
        This Is The Place, W32
        Voudoun, W250

1960   *From Far Away*, W251
        Kuthara, W157
        Old Black Levee, W252

1961   *Barcarola* (solo voice), W253
        Hush My Heart (SATB), W185
        Hush My Heart (solo voice), W254
        Hush My Heart (SSAA), W186
        Nisan, W187
        You, W255

1962   *Cosmic Mist Symphony*, W33
        The Dark Lady Within, W158
        In The Beginning, W59
        The Secret, W256

1963   *Awake to Life* (chorus), W188
        Four Sarabandes (solo piano), W118
        Harvest Heritage, W189
        Kambu (ballet), W159
        Kambu (orchestra), W34
        Little per cent, W35

1964   *Brothers of the Clouds* (chorus and orchestra), W191
        Brothers of the Clouds (chorus and piano), W190
        Eternal Spirit (chorus), W192
        Eternal Spirit (solo voice), W257
        Lullaby of the Bells, W258
        Western Testament, W160

1965   *The Builders* (chorus and piano), W193
       The Builders (solo voice and piano), W259
       Cactus Rhapsody (two pianos), W145
       Les Fameux Douze (The Famous Twelve) (solo piano), W119
       Les Fameux Douze (The Famous Twelve) (small orchestra), W36
       The Flute Song, W194
       Four Sarabandes (woodwind quintet), W60
       In Silence of the Temple, W195
       Reflection, W146

1966   *Anima Divina,* W147
       Epiphyllum (solo piano), W120
       Les Fameux Douze (The Famous Twelve) (violin and cello), W61
       Ridin' Herd in Texas, W121

1967   *Alaskan Trail of '98* (solo piano), W122
       Casa Blanca by the Sea, W260
       Elvina de la Luz, W261
       Have I Told You, W262
       Pastorale (recorder, oboe and harpsichord), W62

1968   *Awake to Life* (brass quintet), W63

1969   *Egyptian Suite,* W123
       Holy Lullaby (chorus), W196
       Holy Lullaby (solo voice), W263
       Processional, W64
       Recessional, W65

1970   *Forest Procession,* W197
       Lakalani, W124
       Overtones, W264
       Phantasy (flute and piano), W66
       The Ten Commandments, W198
       Translunar Cycle (solo voice), W265

1971   *The Builders* (chorus and orchestra), W199
       Earth Mother (chorus), W200
       Earth Mother (solo voice), W266
       Hawaiian Chants: Pianorama of Hawai'i, W125
       Ka Nani O Ka Lani (chorus), W201
       Ka Nani O Ka Lani (solo voice), W267
       Little Man (chorus), W202
       Lord, God Within Me (solo voice), W268
       My Dream, W269
       Pyramids of Giza (organ), W148
       Song of the Heart (chorus), W203
       A Tribute, W270

1972   *Lotusland*, W271
          Song of the Heart (solo voice), W272

1973   *Pyramids of Giza* (orchestra), W37

1974   *Phantasy* (woodwind trio), W67

1975   *The Earth Does Not Wish for Beauty* (TTBB), W204
          The Earth Does Not Wish for Beauty (voice, 2 trumpets, horn,
             trombone and tuba), W68
          Pastorale (flute and harp), W69
          Rhumbando (wind ensemble), W70

1976   *Adoration* (two trumpets, horn and trombone), W71
          Hebraic Poem, W72

1977   *Cactus Rhapsody* (clarinet, cello and piano), W73
          Cherokee Blessing, W205
          The Earth Does Not Wish for Beauty (four tubas), W74
          Invocation, W126
          Kuilima, W127
          Lord, God Within Me (chorus), W206

1978   *Lei of Love*, W128
          Lord Have Mercy, W207
          Love Song, W273

1979   *Dance Grotesque* (flute and piano), W75
          Prison (Lament) (string quartet), W76
          Weep Not, W274

1980   *Alaskan Trail of '98* (band), W38
          Fulfillment, W275
          I Found a Star, W276
          Love Still Has Something of the Sea (chorus), W208
          Translunar Cycle (cello and piano), W77

1981   *AdáKris*, W129
          Anwar Sadat (solo piano), W130
          Ode to NASA, W78
          Saint Francis of Assisi (organ), W149
          We Are The Wind Chimes, W277

1982   *After the Storm*, W131
          Anwar Sadat (In Memory) (orchestra), W39
          Lost River, W278
          Mother (A Melody of Love) (voice and orchestra), W280
          Mother (A Melody of Love) (voice and piano), W279

1983   *Alaskan Inner Passage,* W132
       Surf and Sand, W133

1984   *Earth of God* (orchestra), W40
       Earth of God (solo piano), W134
       Soul of the Sea, W79

1985   *Neutrinos,* W135
       O Sing Unto The Lord, W209
       Upbeat (solo piano), W136

1986   *Sam Houston* (solo piano), W137

1987   *Epiphyllum* (solo piano, left hand), W138
       Sam Houston (orchestra), W41
       Texas, W42

1988   *Upbeat* (solo piano, third grade), W139

1989   Suite for String Quartet, W80

Appendix II:
Alphabetical List of Works

Adákris (1981), W129
Adoration [solo piano] (1955), W114
   Adoration [two trumpets, horn and trombone] (1976), W71
After the Storm (1982), W131
Alaskan Inner Passage (1983), W132
Alaskan Trail of '98 [solo piano] (1967), W122
   Alaskan Trail of '98 [band] (1980), W38
All Alone on the Prairie (1945), W238
Angel Chimes [solo piano] (1951), W106
   Angel Chimes [two pianos] (1951), W142
   Angel Chimes [orchestra] (1954), W28
Anima Divina (1966), W147
Anwar Sadat [solo piano] (1981), W130
   Anwar Sadat (In Memory) [orchestra] (1982), W39
Awake To Life [chorus] (1963), W188
   Awake To Life [brass quintet] (1968), W63

Baby I Can't Sleep [solo voice] (1936), W222
   Baby I Can't Sleep [chorus] (1936), W170
Barcarola [violin and piano] (1948), W54
   Barcarola [solo piano] (1948), W98
   Barcarola [chorus] (1949), W179
   Barcarola [eight celli and vocalise] (1958), W57
   Barcarola [solo voice] (1961), W253
Berceuse (1927), W216
Brothers of the Clouds [chorus and piano] (1964), W190
   Brothers of the Clouds [chorus and orchestra] (1964), W191
The Builders [chorus and piano] (1965), W193
   The Builders [voice and piano] (1965), W259
   The Builders [chorus and orchestra] (1971), W199

Cactus Rhapsody [solo piano] (1953), W109
  Cactus Rhapsody [orchestra] (1953), W27
  Cactus Rhapsody [two pianos] (1965), W145
  Cactus Rhapsody [clarinet, cello, piano] (1977), W73
Canyon [piano sketch] (1939), W88
  Canyon [orchestra] (1939), W10
Carillon (1952), W155
Casa Blanca By The Sea (1967), W260
Casa del Sogno [violin and piano] (1955), W56
  Casa Del Sogno [oboe and piano] (1958), W58
The Chalice [solo voice] (1948), W241
  The Chalice [chorus] (1951), W180
The Chateau [solo piano] (1938), W86
  The Chateau [violin] (1938), W48
  The Chateau [harp] (1965); see Reflection (1965), W146
Cherokee Blessing (1977), W205
Chicken In The Rough [piano sketch] (1951), W107
  Chicken In The Rough [orchestra] (1951), W26
Chipmunks (1940), W49
Cosmic Mist Symphony (1962), W33
Cowboy Rhapsody (1956), W30

Dance Grotesque [solo piano] (1929), W84
  Dance Grotesque [violin and piano] (1929), W45
  Dance Grotesque [two flutes] (1940), W50
  Dance Grotesque [flute and piano] (1979), W75
Dance of the Clown (1945), W94
The Dark Lady Within (1962), W158
Dicky Donkey [SATB] (1935), W164
  Dicky Donkey [SSAA] (1935), W165
Drouth [orchestra] (1939), W11
  Drouth [solo piano] (1939), W89
Drums of Africa [SATB] (1934), W161
  Drums of Africa [TTBB] (1934), W162

The Earth Does Not Wish for Beauty [solo voice] (1940), W230
  The Earth Does Not Wish for Beauty [SATB and piano] (1940),
    W174
  The Earth Does Not Wish for Beauty [SATB and orchestra] (1953),
    W181
  The Earth Does Not Wish for Beauty [TTBB and piano] (1975),
    W204
  The Earth Does Not Wish for Beauty [voice, 2 trumpets, horn,
    trombone and tuba] (1975), W68
  The Earth Does Not Wish for Beauty [four tubas] (1977), W74
Earth Mother [chorus] (1971), W200
  Earth Mother [solo voice] (1971), W267
Earth of God [solo piano] (1984), W134
  Earth of God [orchestra] (1984), W40

Egyptian Suite (1969), W123
Elegy (1937), W223
Elvina de la Luz (1967), W261
Enchantment (1949), W101
Ensenada (1956), W115
Epic Poem; see *Portrait of Thomas Jefferson*
Epiphyllum [solo piano] (1966), W120
  Epiphyllum [piano, left hand] (1987), W138
Escape (1949), W102
Eternal Cycle (1942), W234
Eternal Spirit [chorus] (1964), W192
  Eternal Spirit [solo voice] (1964), W257
Explorations; see *Sonata, Op. 17*

Fairy of Spring (1935), W166
Les Fameux Douze (The Famous Twelve) [small orchestra] (1965),
    W36
  Les Fameux Douze (The Famous Twelve) [solo piano] (1965), W119
  Les Fameux Douze (The Famous Twelve) [violin and cello] (1966),
    W61
Farewell at Dawn (1949), W244
The Flute Song (1965), W194
Forest Procession (1970), W197
Four Sarabandes [solo piano] (1963), W118
  Four Sarabandes [woodwind quintet] (1965), W60
Franciscan Sketches; see *Saint Francis of Assisi*, W17 and *San Luis
  Rey*, W18
From Far Away (1960), W251
Fulfillment (1980), W275

Geppetto's Toy Shop (1940), W90
Goddess of Inspiration [solo voice] (1948), W242
  Goddess of Inspiration [solo piano] (1948), W99

Had I A Cave (1925), W210
Hail Texas (1927), W217
Half Rising Moon (1925), W211
Happyland (1946), W153
Harvest Heritage (1963), W189
Haunted (1935), W167
Have I Told You (1967), W262
Hawaiian Chants: Pianorama of Hawai'i (1971), W125
Hebraic Poem (1976), W72
Heel and Toe (1949), W103
Heroic Poem (1929), W3
Holy Lullaby [solo voice] (1969), W263
  Holy Lullaby [chorus] (1969), W196
How to Play the Piano (1950), W105
Humble Me (1941), W177

Hush My Heart [SATB] (1961), W185
   Hush My Heart [SSAA] (1961), W186
   Hush My Heart [solo voice] (1961), W254

I Found a Star (1980), W276
Immortality [solo voice] (1926), W212
   Immortality [chorus] (1937), W171
Infant Suite [solo piano] (1935), W85
   Infant Suite [small orchestra] (1935), W6
In Living Ecstasy [voice and piano] (1938), W224
   In Living Ecstasy [voice and orchestra] (1938), W225
In Silence of the Temple (1965), W194
Intermezzo (1950), W55
In The Beginning (1962), W59
Invocation (1977), W126
I'se Comin' Lord to You (1940), W175

Jewels of Lake Tahoe (1945), W21
Joy (1953), W110
The Juggler (1948), W100

Kambu [ballet] (1963), W159
   Kambu [orchestra] (1963), W34
Ka Nani O Ka Lani [solo voice] (1971), W267
   Ka Nani O Ka Lani [chorus] (1971), W201
Kuilima (1977), W127
Kuthara (1960), W157

Lady in the Dark; see *The Dark Lady Within*
Lakalani (1970), W124
Lament; see *Prison*
Lasso Of Time [solo voice] (1940), W231
   Lasso Of Time [chorus] (1940), W176
Legend (1928), W44
Lei of Love (1978), W128
Life's Ebb and Flow (1941), W233
Light (1935), W7
Little Man [solo voice] (1951), W246
   Little Man [chorus] (1971), W202
Little per cent (1963), W35
Little Spaniard (1938), W87
Lord, God Within Me [solo voice] (1971), W268
   Lord, God Within Me [chorus] (1977), W206
Lord Have Mercy (1978), W207
Lost River (1982), W278
Lotusland (1972), W271
Love Me Today (1942), W235
Love Song (1978), W273
Love Song of the Taj Mahal (1947), W240

Love Still Has Something Of the Sea [solo voice] (1952), W247
   Love Still Has Something Of The Sea [chorus] (1980), W208
Lullaby of the Bells (1964), W258

Mexican Weaver (1954), W113
Minha Terra (Barrozo Netto) [two pianos] (1956), W143
   Minha Terra (Barrozo Netto) [orchestra] (1958), W31
More Rain, More Rest (1945), W239
Mother (A Melody of Love) [voice and piano] (1982), W279
   Mother (A Melody of Love) [voice and orchestra] (1982), W280
My Dream (1971), W269

Nature Ushers in the Dawn (1939), W173
Neutrinos (1985), W135
Nirvana (1927), W218
Nisan (1961), W187
Nocturn for Small Orchestra (1934), W5
Noontide (1935), W168
"Nostalgia;" <u>see</u> Suite for Strings

Ocean Moods (1925), W81
Ode to NASA (1981), W78
Old Black Levee (1960), W252
Ontonagon Sketches (1939), W12
Open the Door To Me [voice and piano] (1926), W213
   Open the Door To Me [voice and orchestra] (1939), W229
O Sing Unto The Lord (1985), W209
Overtones (1970), W264
Overture to *Pygmalion;* <u>see</u> *Prelude To A Drama*

Paint Horse and Saddle [piano sketch] (1947), W97
   Paint Horse and Saddle [orchestra] (1947), W25
Pastorale [orchestra] (1939), W13
   Pastorale [two pianos] (1939), W140
   Pastorale [recorder, oboe and harpsichord] (1967), W62
   Pastorale [flute and harp] (1975), W69
Le Petit Concerto (1957), W144
Phantasy [oboe and piano] (1942), W51
   Phantasy [oboe, harp and piano] (1942), W52
   Phantasy [oboe and orchestra] (1942), W19
   Phantasy [flute and piano] (1970), W66
   Phantasy [woodwind trio (clarinet, oboe and bassoon)] (1974), W67
Portrait of Thomas Jefferson (1927), W43
Prayer (1934), W163
Prelude (1925), W82
Prelude To A Drama (1928), W1

Prison (Lament) [violin and piano] (1935), W47
  Prison (Lament) [Russian instruments] (1935), W8
  Prison (Lament) [small orchestra] (1940), W15
  Prison (Lament) [string quartet] (1979), W76
Processional (1969), W64
Pyramids of Giza [organ] (1971), W148
  Pyramids of Giza [orchestra] (1973), W37

Radiation; see *Solar Joy*
Rain (1935), W169
Recessional (1969), W65
Red Clay [orchestra] (1946), W22
  Red Clay [solo piano] (1946), W95
  Red Clay [ballet] (1950), W154
Reflection [harp] (1965), W146
Reflections [solo piano] (1953), W111
Requiem (1929), W219
Revelation (1958), W249
Rhapsodic Phantasie [orchestra] (1933), W4
  Rhapsodic Phantasie [two pianos] (1950), W141
"Rhumbando"; see *Southern Symphony*
Rhumbando (1975), W70
Ridin' Herd in Texas (1966), W121

Saint Francis of Assisi [orchestra] (1941), W17
  Saint Francis of Assisi [solo piano] (1941), W92
  Saint Francis of Assisi [organ] (1981), W149
Sam Houston [solo piano] (1986), W137
  Sam Houston [orchestra] (1987), W41
San Luis Rey [orchestra] (1941), W18
  San Luis Rey [solo piano] (1941), W93
Saturnale (1939), W14
The Secret (1962), W256
Serenada Del Coronado (1940), W91
Serenade [solo voice] (1942), W236
  Serenade [violin and piano] (1944), W53
Serenata Sorrentina [orchestra] (1946), W23
  Serenata Sorrentina [solo piano] (1946), W96
Shepherd in the Distance (1929), W150
Silver Wings (1942), W237
Soil Magic (1955), W248
Solar Joy [solo piano] (1953), W112
  Solar Joy [orchestra] (1955), W29
Sonata, Op. 17 (1958), W117
Song of the Heart [chorus] (1971), W203
  Song of the Heart [solo voice] (1972), W272
Song of the Joshua (1956), W116
Soul Of The Sea (1984), W79
Southern Symphony (1935), W9

The Spider and the Butterfly (1953), W156
The Star and the Child [SATB] (1956), W182
  The Star and the Child [SSA] (1956), W183
Stillness [solo voice] (1940), W232
  Stillness [chorus] (1941), W178
String Quartet (1934), W46
Suite for Strings (1940), W16
  Suite for String Quartet (1989), W80
Sunken City [voice and piano] (1926), W214
  Sunken City [voice and orchestra] (1938), W226
Surf and Sand (1983), W133
Symphonic Intermezzo (1928), W2

The Ten Commandments (1970), W198
Texas (1987), W42
This Is The Place (1958), W32
Torillo (1949), W104
Translunar Cycle [solo voice] (1970), W265
  Translunar Cycle [cello and piano] (1980), W77
A Tribute (1971), W270
Twilight Moon [solo voice] (1938), W227
  Twilight Moon [chorus] (1938), W172
  Twilight Moon [solo voice and orchestra] (1938), W228

Ubiquity (1937), W152
Umpqua Forest (1946), W24
Upbeat [solo piano] (1985), W136
  Upbeat [solo piano, third grade] (1988), W139

Venete, Felii Audite Me (1957), W184
Vision of Loveliness (1948), W243
Voudoun (1958), W250

The Wanderer's Evening Song (1933), W220
We Are the Wind Chimes (1981), W277
We Believe (1942), W20
Weep Not (1979), W274
Western Suite (1925), W83
Western Testament (1964), W160
Wheel of Life (1933), W151
When We Shall Part (1934), W221
Wings of Silver (1951), W108
Withered Flowers (1926), W215
"Woods at Dusk"; <u>see</u> *Ontonagon Sketches*

You (1961), W255
Your Hand (1949), W245

Index

About the Authors

WALTER B. BAILEY is Associate Professor at Rice University's Shepherd School of Music, Houston, Texas.

NANCY GISBRECHT BAILEY is an instructor for a number of adult education programs in Houston.